ROGER STE P9-CQX-249

APRIL, 1993

The Politics of
Food

The Politics of Food

by
Joel Solkoff

Sierra Club Books · San Francisco

The Fund for Investigative Journalism provided grant money for some of the research reported in this book.

Library of Congress Cataloging in Publication Data
Solkoff, Joel.
    The politics of food.

    Includes index.
    1. Agriculture and state—United States. 2. United States. Dept. of Agriculture. I. Title.
HD1761.S76 1985   338.1'873   85-2119
ISBN 0-87156-846-2

Jacket design by Paul Bacon
Printed in the United States of America
10 9 8 7 6 5 4 3 2 1

*This book is dedicated to my mother
Miriam Pell Schmerler.*

Contents

Acknowledgements

For a certain kind of help that cannot be expressed, I thank my wife Diana and our daughter Joanna Marie.

For their friendship and assistance through all the drafts and for listening to me talk for hours on end about the Sugar Act of 1948 (as amended), rice fields in Arkansas, commodity futures trading, and whatever agriculture policy madness afflicted me without notice at 8:45 on a Saturday night when we were simply going out for a pizza, I thank David F. Phillips and Andrew Jay Schwartzman.

For patiently contributing to my agriculture education year in and year out, I thank William Gahr and all Gahr's employees at the Food Group of the General Accounting Office who without warning were called upon to explain *parity* or modularization of food containers or soil erosion or whatever subject on which I needed educating, and I thank Phillip Moery, who taught me about the bottom line in agriculture—both financially and politically.

For creating this book, I thank Robin Mayers, who read and argued with me about every word; the late Marie Rodell, my agent, who before she died was pleased to see me settled down and working on this project, who couldn't quite believe that she'd ever have a client call her from Stuttgart, Arkansas ("Rice and duck calling capital of the world"), and who counseled me to keep my opinions of pesticides to myself when farmers were kind enough to let me see their farms, and whose concern about pesticides led her to support and make possible a wider audience for Rachel Carson; my agent Frances Collin, of the Marie Rodell-Frances Collin Literary Agency, for her belief in this book; Daniel Moses, of Sierra Club Books, whose quiet perseverance coaxed me to let go of this book (even though it will never really be ready because of a new development which might mean....); and my copy editor Mary Lou Van Deventer who made my prose less difficult to read and whose persistent questioning about why I did not write more about ecology and less about how nifty the commodities market is made me reexamine my motiviation for writing this book.

The remainder of my thanks I cannot adequately categorize; so I thank: The District of Columbia public library system, especially the Martin Luther King Memorial Library and the West End, Southeast, and Northeast branches; the Library of Congress, the congressional research service, the reference librarians at the Library of Congress, especially those who staff the telephones and the main floor reading room, all those anonymous gophers who brought down books of statistics when I'm sure they wished for more exciting searches; the USDA libraries, both the reading room downtown and the National Agriculture Library in Beltsville, Maryland; the scores of experts on agriculture at USDA who through the years put aside their other duties to tell me how many bushels of corn were in carryover, how many migrants did agricultural work in six given counties in California in the month of March, and other statistical questions, including questions on elementary mathematics; all the mathematics teachers I ever had, especially those who taught me the little I had the good sense to retain; the United States Department of Agriculture and the Department of Health, Education, and Welfare and its offspring Health and Human Services; the Departments of Labor, Commerce, Treasury, State, Transportation, and Energy and the Office of the Special Trade Representative, the Environmental Protection Agency, Federal Trade Commission, Securities and Exchange Commission, and the Commodity Futures Trading Commission; the White House press office under the administrations of Richard M. Nixon, Gerald R. Ford, Jimmy Carter, and Ronald Reagan; the Congress of the United States and especially the House and Senate Agriculture committees; the House and Senate periodical press galleries; Howard Bray of the Fund for Investigative Journalism for his continual encouragement and the Fund for its support; *The New Republic, The New York Times, Skeptic,* et al. for publishing and republishing my articles on agricultural policy; Patric Mullen for buying me Bloody Marys, introducing me to members of Congress, and for his friendship; the Media Access Project; Linda Lazarus; *The Washington Post* library and Dan Morgan, Jody Allen, and Michael Barone; the *National Journal* library and especially Robert J. Samuelson; Michael P. Andrews; my mother Miriam P. Schmerler; my father Isadore; my grandmother Celia Pell; my sister Sarah Schmerler; Alvin and Theresa Demick and *Arts Magazine*; Craig Berrington; Jack Brock; the Migrant Legal Action Program; Cesar Chavez, Earl Butz, Hubert H. Humphrey, Dick Clark, William Proxmire, Thomas Foley, David Bowen, and others who granted me interviews; Paul Boertlein; Werner Brandt; former Under Secretary of Labor Robert J. Brown for his encouragement and friendship; David Brody; Ben Simpson of Capitol Hill Gulf; Central Delivery Service; Morris M. Cohen; National Public Radio; Miriam Daniel-Wolff; Susan Dankoff Menick; Michael and Robin Demick; Norman and Phyllis Demick; Julie Dillingham and her family; Theodore F. Brophy; Helen Ericson and the *Journal of Commerce*; Marcia, Barnet, Jonah, and Lee Eskin; my lawyer Susan Chaires; Colin Frank; Richard Gilmore; Jack Halpert; the Japan Uni Agency and especially Tatsuko Nagasawa and Yoshio Taketomi; Robert Leahy; Norma Lewin; Lee Avery Rosenhouse; Gary

Lucken; Barbara Machtiger; Lynn McReynolds; Jonathan Miller of *Communications Daily*; Linda B.R. Mills; Lisa, Sophy, and Phillipa Moery; David Mont; Donald, Michele, Katherine, and Peter Moore; Eunice, Janice, and Kevin Alexander; Curtis T. White and Andrea Engler; Howard Simister and Judith Soderholm; the gang on E Street; the Capitol Hill Baby Sitting Cooperative; David Moyer of Paul Stafford Associates; Agnes Mravcak; Lynne Murphy; David Schneiderman; Wendy Moonan; the National Association of Housing and Redevelopment Officials; the Office of Technology Assessment and its Food Group; the National Press Club; Andrew L. Rothman; Dorothy Row; Cathy Kouts of Sierra Club Books; Edward Sacks; Amiel Segal, among other things for saving my life; Donald Hutter; Paul Bresnick; Eileen Shanahan; Ida Solkoff; Benjamin and Lil Solkoff; Leon and Gerda Zolko; Rona, Joe, and Allison Spiegel; Stationers Inc. of Richmond, Virginia, for making the reporters notebooks I carry everywhere; Diana McLellan, "The Ear"; David Sanford; Deborah Matz; Rita Jenrette; the Legal Services Corporation; Roger Rosenblatt; Martin Peretz; Eliot Marshall; Robert J. Myers; Michael Kinsley; Philip Terzian; the late John Osborne; Leslie B. Seagrave; Gwen Somers; Joan Tapper; Raphael Sagalyn; Paul S. Weisberg, for worrying about this book as if it were his; Jack Raher; Jack Limpert of *The Washingtonian*; Walter Shapiro; Donald Dunnington; Zookie Bass Solkoff; Betty, Jeff, and Elizabeth Laxague; the farmers in California, Arkansas, Louisiana, Arizona, Virginia, Florida, Maryland, North Carolina, Vermont, Massachusetts, and other states who took me around their operations and answered lots of questions; the Chicago Board of Trade, the Chicago Mercantile Exchange, the New York Coffee & Sugar Exchange, and other futures and cash markets for giving me permission to see the action on the floor (even when I sometimes got in the way); the People's Republic of China; the staff of the Joint Economic Committee of Congress;

the late Frank Norris; Calvin Beale, USDA's population guru; the U.S. Sugar Corporation; *The Palm Beach Post*; the government of Jamaica; the United Farm Workers Union; the International Brotherhood of Teamsters Chauffeurs Warehousemen & Helpers; former Secretaries of Agriculture Clifford Hardin and Bob Bergland; the Continental Grain Company; Cook Industries; the Bunge Corporation; William Robbins; Worldwatch Institute; Commodity News Service; Michael Jacobson and the Center for Science in the Public Interest; the United Nations; *Business Week*; the staff at CARE; *The Wall Street Journal*; the brokers at Conti Commodity Services, at Merrill Lynch, Pierce, Fenner & Smith, et al.; the *Des Moines Register*, especially its Washington bureau chief James Risser; former Rep. Fred Richmond; Marc Grossman; the library of *The Los Angeles Times*; *The Yuma [Arizona] Daily Sun*; the National Farmers Union; Riceland Foods; the National Association of Wheat Growers; the American Farm Bureau Federation; the National Grange; the National Farmers Organization; Rural America Inc.; Rodale Press; Secretary of Agriculture John Block; Senator Bob Dole; the American Agriculture Movement; the American Bankers Association; former Sen. Herman Talmadge; former Rep. W.R. Poage; Sen. Edward Kennedy; *Congressional Quarterly*, especially Elizabeth Wehr, its first-rate agriculture reporter, and Hank Donnelly; Catherine Nicholson; Allison Masson; Yukiko Mori; Peter Hannaford; Michael Chinworth; Jun Fushimi, and the many others who through choice or misadventure remain anonymous.

The Politics of
Food

Introduction

> For according to the universal law of events, every
> increase is followed by decrease, and all fullness is
> followed by emptiness.... Abundance can endure
> only if larger groups are brought to share in it, for
> only then can the movement continue without turn-
> ing into its opposite.
>
> —*Book of Changes*

Agriculture is more boring than it used to be but less boring than it seems. Agriculture used to be exciting from 1972 to 1976, when Earl Butz served as secretary of agriculture under presidents Richard Nixon and Gerald Ford. It was exciting because for the first time in recent memory the United States had difficulty supplying enough food to its own citizens, as well as to the rest of the world.

There were widespread predictions (the events did not materialize) that famine and starvation would reach epic proportions, that on the nightly news television viewers in the United States would see Third World scenes of millions of people dying for want of U.S. grain.[1]

Angry consumers—enough of them that they created a potent political movement—demonstrated and boycotted. They protested unexpected increases in food prices, which newspaper headlines described as "skyrocketing." The increases were so consistently high that they helped precipitate an economy dependent on double-digit inflation.

During this period angry anticommunist longshoremen struck and refused to load grain onto ships bound for the Soviet Union. Simultaneously presidents Nixon and Ford, whose political careers were based on lifelong opposition to communism, alternated between virtually begging the Russians to buy U.S. grain and embargoing shipments abroad for fear that the United States would run out of food.

Earl Butz, the most controversial secretary of agriculture in U.S. history, helped make an exciting period even more exciting. Unfortunately Butz has come to be remembered, to the extent that he is remembered at all, for two unrelated events that drove him from office and put him in jail. In 1976 he was forced to resign after the press learned that he had told an obscene and racist "joke." In 1981 he served 25 days in jail (released five days early for good behavior) because he deliberately failed to report $148,000 in taxable income.

Although no excuse is made for the considerable defects in Butz's character, Earl Butz was a powerful secretary of agriculture whose ideas still affect the world's food policy today. Some experts argue that the principal agricultural problems in the United States and throughout the world stem from Butz's policies. Others argue that the problems have arisen because subsequent governmental decision-makers failed to adhere to the free-market principles Butz espoused and wrote into the law. In any case, no one can talk rationally about U.S. agricultural policy in the 1980s, and probably for the remainder of the century, without discussing the changes Butz made.

Butz's power as secretary of agriculture seemed overwhelming. He made one decision—to sell the Russians massive quantities of grain—that virtually overnight transformed the basic problem of U.S. agricultural policy from what to do with the surplus to how to make up for the shortage. Before him, agricultural policy was dominated by the fact that the United States produced more food than it could possibly sell, give away, and store. Farmers prayed for bad weather, especially on their neighbors' land, so that supply would go down, prices would go up, and their income would no longer depend on government payments. Even when bad weather struck, however, it failed to destroy enough crops to solve the problems caused by surplus.

After so significantly changing the agricultural economy, Butz found overhauling the country's agricultural laws relatively easy. His predecessors considered it a legislative victory to change a few words and paragraphs in the farm laws, but they left the body of law basically unaltered since it had been created in the early 1930s. Butz rewrote some laws and abolished others, dismantling a system of land controls and subsidies that restricted able farmers and rewarded the others for their inefficiency.

Although he had problems with directors of management and budget, as well as with Henry Kissinger and other officials who wanted to use agricultural exports as a weapon in U.S. foreign policy, Butz seemed to have a power of his own. President Nixon, had he cared, was too involved in the Watergate crisis (among other things) to do anything about farm policy. President Ford didn't care. Thus Earl Butz rewrote the country's farm laws without the interference experienced by secretaries of agriculture serving under presidents Jimmy Carter and Ronald Reagan.

Surprisingly Butz, a Republican, ushered his laws through a Democratic Congress despite the active opposition of congressional farm leaders, including the chairs of the House and Senate agricultural committees. Both Bob Bergland and John Block, secretaries of agriculture under presidents Carter and Reagan respectively, had difficulty passing comparatively minor legislation even though Democrat Bergland was working with a Democratic Congress and Republican Block with a Republican Senate.

Butz was able to "get the government out of agriculture," as he had promised. Before his tenure, decisions on how much a farmer could plant were made in the office of the secretary of agriculture in Washington, D.C. He changed the location of these decisions to the commodity pits at the Chicago Board of Trade and other exchanges. After his tenure, farmers became confused about where to go for direction, because the government reentered the policy-making process in an unpredictable, unthinking way.

After 1976 Earl Butz's legislative accomplishments and the market-oriented ideology they implemented appeared to fade. Butz's policies were powerless to prevent abundance from returning to farms throughout the world. Subsequent secretaries of agriculture did not understand why the transition to abundance was taking place. They tried to protect farmers while simultaneously keeping U.S. farm policy out of the government's control; they failed at both objectives. They were working with a confused and sometimes frightened Congress and with presidents who did not let them do their jobs. They were powerless as Congress passed laws that were confusing and expensive. In fact, after the omnibus 1981 farm bill was passed, it did not work. This law, which expires in 1985, did exactly the opposite of what it was intended to do.

Agriculture is not as exciting as it once was because after 1976 its principal problem changed from shortage to surplus. It is more interesting to read an account of how people were rescued at the last minute from starving to death—which happened all too frequently during Earl Butz's tenure—than to read about how hard it was for lackluster secretaries Bergland and Block to store huge surpluses of wheat.[2]

Agriculture is not as boring as it seems because there is no guarantee that this period of surplus will last. No one in government is taking precautions against new global shortages that could reappear through drought, pestilence, or other plagues not even contemplated. One unexpectedly significant disaster occurred in 1973, when the anchovy catch in Peru was inexplicably low. Because anchovies are a significant ingredient in animal feed, an unexpected anchovy shortage occurring simultaneously with an unexpected grain shortage had a surprisingly severe impact on the world's food supply. Today the executive and legislative agricultural decision-makers are intellectual and political lightweights incapable of grasping the major issues that affect how much food U.S. citizens have to eat. From 1976 to the present, America's agricultural policy-makers have not even considered preparing for the future.

Earl Butz's most lasting contribution was to emphasize the importance of food. This importance may seem obvious, but before Butz it never seriously occurred to agricultural policy-makers that America could run out of food. Agriculture was dominated by technical discussions on such issues as allotments, parity, and non-recourse loans. Today policy-makers again seem unaware of how important food is.

This obliviousness is dangerous. Unless the United States replaces ineffective secretaries of agriculture and powerless congressional agricultural committee chairs with competent leaders who understand the issues, the country's current and future food supply is at risk. Pessimism seems unavoidable. After examining the facts, it is impossible to escape the conclusion that America's food policy will not improve until disaster strikes—a disaster for which the country is not prepared.

---

1. Imagine, for example, how much worse would be the current famine in Ethiopia if the U.S. and other nations could not send relief because there were no food available to send.

2. So massive are current surpluses that during the summer of 1984 when the Soviets made one of the largest grain purchases in history, the effect on supply—and indeed on price—was slight.

Chapter One

Farmers Don't Live Here Anymore

"Do you know what I have come for?" says Jurgen, blustering and splendid in his glittering shirt and his gleaming armor. "For I warn you I am justice."

"I think you are lying, and I am sure you are making an unnecessary noise. In any event, justice is a word, and I control all words."

—*Jurgen, A Comedy of Justice* by James Branch Cabell

At the end of 1971, when Richard Nixon nominated Earl Butz to be his second secretary of agriculture, the U.S. government was paying farmers over $3 billion a year not to grow corn, wheat, rice, and several other crops. It was also using that money and various legal mechanisms to keep the price of milk, oranges, sugar, meat, tomatoes, and other food artificially high.

Butz's confirmation hearings were the most controversial in the history of the Senate Agriculture Committee. Traditionally confirmation hearings for agriculture secretaries were routine and nonpartisan, conducted in a quiet club-like atmosphere. For example Butz's predecessor, Clifford Hardin, was unanimously confirmed, and the hearing transcript was 11 pages long. The transcript of the Butz hearings before the same committee members ran 212 pages. The event even generated unprecedented television coverage. The confirmation squeaked out of committee by a vote of 8 to 6 and through the Senate by 51 to 44.

The Senate Agriculture Committee was hostile because Butz opposed paying farmers not to grow and because he opposed governmental programs designed to keep farm prices high. His objective, he said, was "to get the government out of agriculture." The hearings introduced the public to the little-known word "agribusiness." Much was made of Butz's service on the board of directors of three *Fortune* 500 companies.[1] At the hearing Democratic Senator Fred Harris of Oklahoma called Butz "an agent of the giant agribusiness corporations that are driving the small farmers of America off the land." Harris said that unless the nomination were stopped, Richard Nixon and Earl Butz would successfully hand over the country's food production to big business.

But Harris and his committee colleagues knew that small farmers had been driven off the land long before, and that our country's food supply was already controlled by a few corporations and corporate-like farmers. Few senators on the committee were really concerned about Butz's presence on the board of three agribusinesses. Most received campaign contributions from agribusinesses and promoted their interests in Congress, including liberals such as Democratic Senator Hubert Humphrey of Minnesota.

Because Butz insisted on saying aloud that agriculture in the U.S. is a business, however, he provoked congressional anger and continued to generate controversy about his farm policies throughout his tenure as secretary. Congressional farm experts didn't disagree with Butz's description of reality, but they were incensed by his indiscretion, afraid that his public honesty might threaten their power. They had been making policy for decades based on the premise that agriculture was not a business. As a result, from November 1971 until Butz resigned in 1976, senators and representatives who knew better unleashed their rhetoric about the danger to the family farm.

An incident from April 1975 illustrates how easy it was for congressional farm experts to get caught up in their own rhetoric. Hubert Humphrey, chairman of the Joint Economic Committee of Congress, was holding hearings on "the entire range of agriculture questions." Senator William Proxmire (a Democrat from Wisconsin) stopped by to complain that the Department of Agriculture was dumping cheese on the market and driving dairy farmers out of business. "Last year we lost 10 farmers a day in our state," he said. An aide whispered, "Most died of old age."

Finally, after hearing nearly three hours of testimony, Humphrey delivered an impassioned speech. "I remember the Depression days when the people that really led the farmers' revolt were not some farmers that had . . . 10 acres . . . and never made a dime, but the leading farm organizer in my part of the country was a fellow by the name of Hanson, who was a pillar in the Lutheran Church and who was one of the most prosperous farmers that we had in there in the 1920s. He was out there leading the parade right down to Campbell Park in 1934. I remember the farmers going down the street with pitchforks and rakes in their hands." Then Humphrey said, "I remember a few hangings. They were Federal judges. I hope that doesn't happen again."

Agriculture Secretary Butz, scheduled to lead off the next round of testimony, was already being fitted for the noose. Humphrey's anger filled the air with excitement and it was easy to imagine how, as the young Democratic-Farmer-Labor mayor of Minneapolis, Humphrey had ignited the 1948 Democratic National Convention. It was only after he banged the gavel and said, "We have to go," that it became apparent the room was empty. Only one reporter was present. Fewer than 10 people heard his remarks.

Decades before the Butz nomination there were few farmers in the United States. By 1971 4.6 percent of the American people lived and worked on farms. More people lived in the cities of New York and Philadelphia than on all the farms in the U.S. There were fewer farmers than unemployed people.

Consequently most Americans did not know where their food came from. By 1971 most people had difficulty locating the nearest farm, could not describe the process involved in producing hamburgers or hamburger rolls, and could not tell where the sugar in their coffee or the rice the United States shipped to East Pakistan came from. Few understood basic biological facts, such as a cow—like all mammals— must be pregnant to give milk, and as a result artificial insemination had become indispensable to milk production. An airplane planting seeds or three workers harvesting a thousand acres of wheat was outside their experience. Few had been to a corn farm in Iowa or had seen rows of machine-planted lettuce in California growing as far as the eye could see.

In 1974 a census report noted that Steele County, North Dakota, had the highest per capita income in the country, and a stand-up comedian boasted he could prove North Dakota did not exist: "Has anyone in the room ever been there?" Even in California, America's most populous state, the rich agricultural valleys were isolated from population centers, and there was little motivation to get off the freeways and visit the farms.

California's Imperial Valley illustrates the isolation. To the northeast lie the Chocolate Mountains, where in the late 1850s advertisements for the stage read, "Passengers are advised to provide themselves with a Sharp's rifle and one hundred rounds of ammunition." The road east goes to Yuma, Arizona, past the desert where Hollywood used to film its French Foreign Legion movies.

To get to the valley, one drives 115 miles due east of San Diego along Interstate 8, a multi-lane freeway. Spanish explorers called the route Jornada de la Muerta—Journey of Death. In winter, en route from the 60-degree weather in San Diego to the 73-degree weather in below-sea-level El Centro, one often has to follow snow plows among the

3000-foot peaks of the Penninsula Range, which separates San Diego's congressional representative from the rest of the huge and sparsely populated district. Coming down into the desert, the traveler notices chaparral, yellow-brown rocks, and the barrenness of the countryside.

After getting off the freeway and driving down two-lane Route 98, suddenly one sees a clump of trees and—poof— green! For some 80 miles, hugging the Mexican-American border along the highway marked Border Friendship Route, the All-American Canal brings water from the Colorado River, turning (as an historical marker notes) a "once arid area into an agricultural paradise." Nowhere in the United States is the importance of water more obvious than in this valley, which has an annual rainfall of 3.2 inches. The federal government helped finance more than 3200 miles of canals and irrigation ditches—the largest irrigation project in the world—that turned a half-million acres of desert into fertile land.

By 1969 Imperial had become the fourth richest agricultural county in the nation, supplying most eastern states' winter lettuce, and by 1975 it was also selling $8.8 million a year in asparagus, $2.9 million in watermelons, $57.2 million in sugar beets, $43.2 million in wheat, and $122 million in cattle. Like the even richer counties farther north, Imperial can grow virtually every commercial crop in its irrigated soil.

"Nobody comes to Imperial County just to see Imperial County," the wife of a county agricultural official said at the Mid-Winter Fair. Few visitors just pass through.

"This farming town is the 'carrot capital' of the world," sports columnist Dave Anderson later wrote from Holtville. "Bugs Bunny should train here instead of baseball players." Except for baseball players, drug smugglers, army bomb testers, illegal aliens on the run, and people who love the desert, agriculture is the only reason for being in the Imperial Valley.

In addition to being isolated geographically, by 1971

farms had become removed from America's consciousness. Most Americans still thought of a farm according to the Old MacDonald stereotype, with some wheat here, cows there, apple trees elsewhere, and a Grant Wood family working together in bucolic bliss. Although such places still existed, it had been decades since they supplied a significant percentage of our nation's food. In 1972 there were a total of 2.9 million farms in the U.S.; the 1 million largest ones provided 90 percent of America's food. The *average* farm was 382 acres and getting larger. By 1976, according to one estimate, a farmer had to have at least 3000 acres of wheat or 1000 acres of corn to afford a tractor. Farmland in Iowa was selling for $2000 an acre. A $6-million operation was not what most Americans thought of when they heard about the plight of the family farm.

By 1972 deploring the corporate nature of American agriculture had become a long-standing tradition. In the 1906 novel *The Octopus*, one of Frank Norris' heroines "remembered the days of her young girlhood passed on a farm in eastern Ohio — five hundred acres, neatly partitioned into the water lot, the cow pasture, the corn lot, the barley field, and wheat farm, cosey [sic], comfortable, homelike; where the farmers loved their land, caressing it, coaxing it, nourishing it as though it were a thing almost conscious; where the seed was sown by hand, and a single two-horse plough was sufficient for the entire farm; where the scythe sufficed to cut the harvest and the grain was thrashed with flails.

"But this new order of things — a ranch bounded only by the horizons, where, as far as one could see, to the north, to the east, to the south, and to the west, was all one holding, a principality ruled with iron and steam, bullied into a yield of three hundred and fifty thousand bushels . . . troubled her and even at times filled her with an undefinable terror. To her mind there was something inordinate about it all, something almost unnatural. The direct brutality of ten thousand acres of wheat, nothing but wheat as far as the eye could see, stunned her a little. The one-time writing-teacher of a young ladies' seminary . . . shrank from it. She did not want to look at so much wheat. There was something vaguely indecent in the sight, this food of the people, this elemental force, this basic energy, weltering here under the sun in all the unconscious nakedness of a sprawling, primordial Titan."

During the 1970s there were only 4.4 million farmers, hired hands, seasonal farmworkers, and migrants working on all the farms in the nation. The same California Norris described was producing a quarter of America's food. More than 15 percent of its farms had payrolls larger than $20,000 a year. United Brands, a New York-based conglomerate, owned the largest lettuce farm in the country, California's InterHarvest, and farmed a total of 22,000 acres in California and Arizona. Tenneco, a corporation with interests in everything from natural-gas pipelines to automotive components, farmed 1.4 million acres in California and Arizona.

Even many farms defined as "family farms" were corporate in nature. For example, a third of all the wine the United States consumed was produced in California on the 3500-acre "family farm" owned by Ernest and Julio Gallo. Many family farmers were members of large agricultural cooperatives, which controlled the marketing and price of such commodities as rice, cranberries, lettuce, and milk. Most fresh oranges came from California and Arizona growers, 70 percent of whom were members of the Sunkist marketing cooperative.

Because so few people lived on farms, and because a farm could extend for thousands of acres, capital-intensive machinery had become indispensable. A 1976 USDA yearbook showed an eight-wheeled tractor that retailed for about $50,000 and had an air-conditioned cab with an AM-FM radio and other special equipment. Owner Ronnie Lyons in Missouri "often spends 12 hours a day driving the tractor."

Because huge tracts of food attract swarms of insects,

agricultural economists argued that without pesticides and herbicides, capital-intensive agriculture would be impossible. Machines sprayed the land with fertilizers and the crops with pesticides and herbicides, and still other machines did the harvesting. Long before 1972 farming had come to resemble an automated factory where few people were needed to produce the product.

Consider, for example, the technology involved in planting rice in southwest Louisiana. It was morning at the Jennings Municipal Airport in Jefferson Davis Parish, which is part of the seventh congressional district, the largest rice-producing district in the country. A group of men talked about the previous night's tornadoes and hauled hundred-pound sacks of seed rice from the rear of a flatbed truck, slit the sacks, and dumped the rice into a large hopper. The loader truck lifted the hopper, with its 2000 pounds of rice, and in less than 10 minutes the seeds were inside the tank of a single-seat Grumman-American AG-Cat airplane, and the plane was aloft.

The seeds were kernels of rice left to soak overnight in a nearby canal. Already little shoots had sprouted from each kernel. Two days before, the rice could have been hulled, milled, and sold for premium prices. It was the best of the previous year's crop, carefully selected; if all went well, a high percentage of the new crop would be long, narrow kernels, white and unbroken when the husks were removed and the bran milled off. Milling tends to break inferior grades' kernels, which stick together and appear mushy. Mushy rice is not where the money is.

The farmers here said they were producing rice for the "American housewife," verbal shorthand for consumers who buy the white rice that lacks most of the minerals, protein, and niacin for which rice is famous and who insist on each cooked kernel being separate and visually attractive. To meet specifications for millable rice, research services of federal and state agriculture departments have developed special varieties, which are also adapted to the climate, soil, and pest conditions of the region. The seed rice in the tank of the Grumman airplane was the product of this research.

It was May Day, and more than 90 percent of the crop had already been planted. The airplane, owned by farmer Ed Krielow, flew low over fields already green and high from an early March planting. The rush was on to get the final seed in the ground.

The pilot swooped low over a rectangle flooded with water, a rice paddy or "field" with tractor-made levees poking up from the water's surface. Two men stood on opposite sides of the field holding white flags in their hands to tell the pilot where to plant the seeds.

The plane flew so close to the water that there were only inches to spare. Little ripples appeared. "Do you see the seeds?" Ed Krielow asked, but in the excitement the observer didn't know what to look at. There were ripples, but the plane looked as if it was about to crash into the telephone poles and electric wires as it turned around and went back into the rice field.

Ed Krielow said, dismissing the danger, "You should see that boy flying when we spray Stam [weed killer]. His wheels graze right on the levees." This was not especially reassuring, but this time the observer knew where to look. Plane. A white shower of seeds. Ripples. "See?" he said. "That was the seed we saw loaded a little while ago." That was how it was possible to plant rice with only three people—a pilot and two fellows holding white flags.

After this factory-like mechanized production of crops on specialized farms, the raw produce often bore little relationship to the finished product. Increasingly the nation ate processed food. By 1972 most fruits and vegetables were either frozen or canned. In 1973 the country's largest cash crop was soybeans, which few Americans eat unprocessed.

In 1976 the largest cash crop was corn, about 80 percent of which was eaten by animals. "Hogs are essentially condensed corn and soybeans," Butz once explained, and he was not joking. Until the 1960s most corn farmers fed corn to their own livestock, and they sold only a third of the crop. The changing economics of specialization required, as one observer explained, "Animals and not crops; crops and not animals." By 1970 55 percent of the corn crop was sold in the marketplace. By 1975 the figure jumped to 64 percent and was increasing at 1 percent a year.

Calvin Beale, in charge of population studies at the U.S. Department of Agriculture (USDA), told of a corn farmer he met in a cafe in Storm Lake, Iowa. "He had gotten out of cattle because he said it doesn't pay unless you have a large feedlot operation. Now he grows nothing but crops on his farm, and with no cattle he works in winter in a job in a local plant. This is in western Iowa in the heart of the Corn Belt. Now, you don't think of that area as having large industry, but there are large meat-processing plants and other factories you wouldn't think were out there, and he said he had no trouble finding work from November until the spring. I asked him what he did and he said he makes parking meters. And he doesn't have a small farm either. With specialization, this is becoming more and more common."

In 1969 there were 985,000 corn farmers in the United States. Considering that the USDA estimated a farmer needs a minimum of 1000 acres to take advantage of modern equipment and technology, not many people had farms large enough to provide them sufficient income. Only 157,000 farmers grew corn on more than 100 acres. By 1974 there were 11 percent fewer corn farmers than in 1969, and large specialized operations increased their domination. For these capital-intensive farmers, high grain prices were necessary to stay in business. For the farmers who produced chicken, milk, beef, eggs, turkey, and pork, corn was important as a raw material. For them, low corn prices were necessary to stay in business.

The reason agricultural policy existed was to provide a balance, so that, for example, grain prices would be high enough that some farmers would produce grain, low enough that other farmers would raise the animals that converted grain into the desired kinds of food, and stable enough that processors and retailers could market products in an orderly way. That policy had been created to prevent the corporate takeover of American farming.

Paradoxically, as corporations and corporate-like organizations succeeded at producing and marketing crops, their takeover of farming provided the balanced, stable prices government policy was supposed to create. It did so by blurring the distinction between producer and processor.

In a process called vertical integration, large companies and agricultural cooperatives took over all production and processing from farming to supermarket. Ralston Purina, for example, not only cleaned and packaged chickens, but it also owned the corn and soybean acreage that grew the Ralston Purina feed that fed the Ralston Purina-owned and -processed chickens. Companies owned farmland, and they leased it and the services of farmers; farmers essentially became managers and skilled laborers who produced raw products. In many parts of the country, if farmers wanted to sell their products, they either had to sign contracts with large companies or to join corporate-like agricultural cooperatives.

By the time Earl Butz became secretary of agriculture, vertical integration accounted for 40 percent of the potatoes Americans ate, 75 percent of processed vegetables, 95 percent of broilers, 70 percent of citrus products, and 33 percent of fresh vegetables. Americans were buying orange juice from Coca-Cola, lettuce from Dow Chemical, Wonder Bread from ITT, and ham from Greyhound. Farming as a way of life in the United States had become a museum-like curiosity, as contemporary as silversmithing, hand printing, and other crafts on display in colonial Williamsburg.

---

1. Clifford Hardin, Butz's predecessor, took Butz's seat on the board of the Ralston Purina Company — a little-noticed event because Hardin avoided controversy.

Chapter Two

It Will Never Be 1933 Again

"I should like to ask the Minister of Agriculture whether in view of the dumping in this country of Japanese pork pies, the right honourable member is prepared to consider a modification of the eight and a half score basic pig from two and a half inches of thickness round the belly as originally specified, to two inches."

Replying for the Minister, the under secretary said: "The matter is receiving the closest attention. As the honourable member is no doubt aware the question of the importation of pork pies is a matter for the Board of Trade, not for the Board of Agriculture. With regard to the specifications of the basic pig, I must remind the honourable member that, as he is doubtless aware, the eight and a half score pig is modelled on the requirements of the bacon curers and has no direct relation to pig meat for sale in pies. That is being dealt with by a separate committee who have not yet made their report."

—*A Handful of Dust*
by Evelyn Waugh

The controversy over Earl Butz's appointment had little to do with Richard Nixon's views about agriculture. Nixon didn't know about agriculture and didn't care, although he routinely expressed the hope—which he believed was vain—that farm program costs be reduced. Later, when soybeans were in short supply, he confessed that he didn't know what a soybean was. Indeed Nixon, like all presidents since FDR, wanted an agriculture secretary who would leave him free to think about more important matters.

Because it had become so specialized, agriculture was routinely handled by the secretary and the appropriate congressional committees. It had been decades since farmers represented a significant percentage of the population, and as a result it had been decades since members of Congress regarded farm issues as important. During the 1970s only one in three members of the House of Representatives was from a "rural" district, and most districts with "rural" labels included significant concentrations of suburban and even urban voters. Rather than learn everything, the House and Senate cast most votes on the advice of congressional experts. Until Earl Butz came along, the complicated farm programs were not regarded as controversial or worth understanding.

Occasionally some incident stimulated the public's interest, such as the Billie Sol Estes scandal, in which mortgages were illegally obtained on nonexistent liquid fertilizer tanks. But generally agricultural policy was left to the specialists. After he became a senator, Robert Dole of Kansas commented on his eight years on the House Agriculture Committee: "After I landed a spot on that committee, I was not certain whether I had been assigned or sentenced." When Shirley Chisholm of New York City was assigned to the House Agriculture Committee, she considered it an insult and indignantly refused to serve. Concerning her appointment to the Forestry Subcommittee, she said, "All the gentlemen know about Brooklyn is that a tree grew there." For years congressional experts, who originally opposed foodstamps, used the program—administered by the USDA—to make sure urban and suburban-based representatives and senators were in town when farm bills came up for a vote.

Butz's nomination therefore posed a special threat to the

handful of agriculture experts in Congress who, for decades, had sat down with the secretary of agriculture and mutually decided the country's agricultural policy.

Senate committee member Fred Harris, who regarded the Senate as a platform for expressing his ideas, was not threatened. Harris was a populist, alerting the country to the need for trust-busting and revitalizing rural America— ideas he knew would not be put to a vote by his colleagues.

But people such as Senate and House Agriculture Committee Chairs Herman Talmadge (a Democrat from Georgia) and Bob Poage (a Democrat from Texas), who made alliances with liberals such as Fred Harris, Hubert Humphrey, and George McGovern (a Democratic senator from South Dakota), were definitely upset. They let other people grab the headlines while they ruled quietly in a genteel style. No secretary of agriculture had ever questioned their view of farm problems.

Butz did so even before his nomination by opposing farm programs. Originally established in 1933, these programs had for decades taken millions of acres of farmland out of production, administered bulging food warehouses, maintained trade barriers, and paid farmers not to grow. Butz's plan was simple. All he had to do was demonstrate that it was no longer 1933. Examination would reveal that since the farmers had left years before, multibillion-dollar programs to keep farmers on the land were a waste of money.

The congressional experts did not want to expose to scrutiny the farm programs that gave them their power. But although they recognized the danger Butz posed, they did not take him seriously, or they would have used their power to defeat the nomination. Instead they incorrectly assumed that if Butz wanted to change the farm laws, he would have to come to them.

They assumed that the unexpected interest in the nomination would die down and the public would return to its indifference. They relied on the seemingly boring and confusing nature of their specialty, convinced that they would have no difficulty stopping Butz, as they had stopped other outsiders, through the slow congressional committee process of hearings, debates, and failure to report bills, and through appeals to tradition.

For example, in 1974 on the floor of the House, Bob Poage defended the Sugar Act by saying, "Aerodynamic engineers cannot tell you how the bumblebee flies, and I cannot tell you how the sugar program functions, but for 40 years it has worked quite well." Poage, who had been in Congress for 37 years and was an expert on the Sugar Act, was invoking a stylized form of congressional modesty: wiser people than we were responsible for our farm policy, so let us trust in the wisdom. Franklin Roosevelt makes sure we will always have enough to eat.

In 1972 the farm programs actually gave the secretary of agriculture considerable power, best illustrated thirty-five miles west of fashionable Palm Beach, Florida. There, in the Everglades country just south of Lake Okeechobee, the federal government paid for a system of dams, flood-control pumps, and canals that drained the swamp water and left a rich black soil, "muck," capable of growing virtually anything. Today it grows expensive sugar instead of cheap vegetables because the secretary of agriculture decreed that it be so.

Belle Glade was the most famous of the Everglades farm towns because of "Harvest of Shame," Edward R. Murrow's classic documentary from 1960 on the plight of migrants who worked there. At the time Florida grew virtually no sugar. In 1960 and 1961, however, presidents Eisenhower and Kennedy decided to bring Castro to his knees by boycotting Cuba's largest crop. So the secretary of agriculture turned the Belle Glade area into the largest sugar-cane-producing region in the continental United States.

By 1972 sugar cane grew on 244 million acres in Florida, even though producing it was more expensive than importing sugar from almost any tropical country in the world,

and even though Jamaicans had to be flown in annually
to harvest the crop by hand. Without governmental subsidies, it would have made more economic sense to grow
anything but sugar there. In 1972 Belle Glade still called
itself the "Winter Vegetable Capital of the World," but by
1975 expanding sugar acreage helped force the area's largest
vegetable producer out of business.

The secretary turned vegetable land into sugar land using
allotments and price supports set up by legislation designed
to keep farmers in business during the Depression. By 1972
there were 151 producers in Florida who received $8.8
million a year from the Department of Agriculture both
for growing and for not growing sugar cane. The biggest
were U.S. Sugar Corp., a public corporation that sold stock
over the counter, and Gulf and Western, a multibillion
dollar conglomerate that manufactured anything from
paper to replacement parts for automobiles. In 1972 U.S.
Sugar Corp. received a check from USDA for $1,836,178.69;
Gulf and Western Food Products received $949,909.67; the
Talisman Sugar Co. received $705,525.33; the New Hope
Sugar Co. received $344,354.73, and A. Duda and Sons,
Inc., received $314,444.83.

President Kennedy's secretary made changes using programs Franklin D. Roosevelt established in 1933 to deal
with the basic problem of American agriculture—surplus.
Farmers didn't produce too much to feed and clothe all the
people in the world, but it was more than enough for people
and countries with money to pay. During the twentieth
century, except for times of war, when we had no trouble
getting rid of what we produced, our nation's rich soil,
advanced farming techniques, and generally favorable
climate produced large surpluses, which kept prices low.
During the Depression low prices year in and year out were
driving farmers out of business.

The obvious solution was to reduce production. If farmers
produced less, then prices would go up. If prices went up,

then so would income. In 1931 Huey Long, the populist governor of Louisiana, pointed out that farmers were growing so much cotton and prices were so low that if planting could be cut back, one year's crop at high prices would give farmers more income than two years' crops at low prices.

But Huey Long did not have the power to stop all cotton farmers, let alone all farmers, from planting. A desperate President Herbert Hoover, who didn't believe he ought to have such power, sent his agriculture secretary around the country urging farmers to "Grow Less, Earn More." Individual farmers were reluctant to plant less, however, for fear their neighbors would take advantage and grow as much as possible, which would put them in an even deeper financial hole and wouldn't help the general price situation. Hoover's voluntary effort failed, and farmers continued to lose their farms.

When Roosevelt became president in 1933 his emergency Agricultural Adjustment Act and subsequent legislation gave the secretary of agriculture the power to force farmers to grow what the government thought should be grown and the power to control the way farmland was used. The measures were controversial. Most people, but especially farmers, dislike being told what to do. Also the public was unsympathetic to farmers who, to eliminate price-lowering surpluses, spilled milk, killed pigs, and destroyed crops during the Depression. The public also disagreed with paying farmers not to plant.

But emergencies are special cases, and Roosevelt took unprecedented power. Even though the Supreme Court declared the Agricultural Adjustment Act and the legislation of 1934 unconstitutional, in 1938 Congress could think of no other solution to the farm problem, so it simply passed again what was essentially the old law. By then the obstructionist judges on the Supreme Court (who had ruled minimum wage, among other things, unconstitutional) had died. Decades later, when Earl Butz became secretary of agriculture, the New Deal legislation was still virtually un-changed and was simply called "our farm program."

Sugar provides a good example for understanding how the Depression-born farm program continued to work. In 1972 there was too much sugar in the world. Many countries, especially lesser-developed ones, wanted to sell sugar to the U.S. at prices lower than our farmers could match and in quantities sufficient to satisfy our needs.

Our farm policy, however, required our government to encourage U.S. farmers to continue producing sugar. Each year the law required the secretary of agriculture to consider the sugar situation in the U.S. and abroad. After doing so, the secretary gave permission to U.S. farmers to plant enough sugar to satisfy half the country's needs for the year. To fill the other half, the secretary allowed other countries to sell to the U.S. Well-enforced quotas prevented too much from entering the country.

Before the crop was even planted, the secretary sat down with his assistants and a variety of complicated charts, fine-tuning the system and deciding what price the government warehouses would pay that year. According to a formula established shortly after World War I when farm prices were high, the price reflected a balance between living costs of farmers and consumers. If the secretary's charts showed the price was still too low to pay farmers' costs, as generally happened, then consumers paid the established price, and the Department of Agriculture made up the difference to cover farmers' costs with farm payments.

Although the law was badly out of date and had lost much of its justification for existing, everyone involved seemed reasonably content. Governments permitted to sell sugar to the United States were pleased because they got higher prices than the world market was paying. In fact, the Dominican Republic, the Philippines, Taiwan, and Peru paid sugar lobbyists in Washington fees reaching $100,000 a year for getting them high quotas. America's sugar farmers were content because they got artificially high prices plus farm payments. Candy manufacturers, soda bottlers, and other processors were content because they got stable, predictable prices. American consumers were content because they had plenty of sugar, and they were not told how much extra the program cost them both directly and indirectly.

Similarly the farm policy required the secretary to consider annually how farmland should be used and how much support would be needed to keep wheat, corn, and other prices high. Then the secretary told people who had permission to be farmers how many acres to plant. Permission to be a farmer was technically called "an allotment." Because the secretary had the power to prevent a farmer who did not have an allotment from selling a crop, a farmer either had an allotment or didn't farm.

Allotments were originally based on the farmer's history of growing a specific crop. During the Depression, a farmer who had been growing corn year in and year out on 500 acres was given a 500-acre allotment—good only for corn. Growing wheat required a specific wheat allotment, and so on. Over the years, the farmer's child or grandchild inherited the allotment along with the farm, or a buyer purchased the allotment along with the farm. The allotment was frequently worth more than the land itself. In some unusual instances a farmer might buy the land from one person and the allotment from someone else.

Having a 500-acre corn allotment did not mean, however, that a farmer could grow corn on all 500 acres. Each planting season the secretary decided how much corn the country needed. If the secretary decided that only 400 acres of a 500-acre allotment should be planted, any farmer who wanted to sell the crop commercially had to let 100 acres lie fallow and collect a government check for not growing. In theory, and occasionally in fact, paying farmers not to grow also helped conserve the soil. In 1972 the system of allotments, based on how land had been used before regulation in the 1930s, was still the foundation for most agricultural policy decisions.

The original objective of our farm policy was to keep farmers on the land. Rather than being made to feel they were receiving handouts from the government, farmers were encouraged to keep up their farming skills. As a consequence, the secretary knew even while establishing the nation's requirements in a given year that frequently there would still be too much produced. For example on the hypothetical 500-acre allotment, the secretary gave permission to grow corn on only 400 acres, knowing at the time that the country would need only 300 acres' worth. So in addition to paying the farmer not to grow on 100 acres, the government also bought 100 acres' worth of surplus and put it into storage bins.

The government justified its purchases of corn, wheat, rice, peanuts, and other commodities[1] by arguing that since agriculture is unpredictable and crops can be wiped out by drought, flood, insects, or other disasters, it is prudent to prepare for an emergency. But decisions on how much to store followed no emergency-preparedness plan. They were entirely based on how much must be taken out of the marketplace to raise prices. By deciding annually how much government warehouses would pay, the secretary directly established prices in addition to helping determine prices by controlling supply.

Internationally the farm program used two basic tactics. For crops the rest of the world often produced more economically — sugar, dairy products, meat, vegetables — quotas and other trade barriers prevented foreign products from entering the U.S. and lowering farm prices. For commodities the U.S. produced in surplus — corn, wheat, rice, cotton, peanuts — this country dumped excess production on the world market, both giving it away and selling it at prices lower than American consumers paid.

By the time Earl Butz took his oath of office, agricultural policy was full of contradictions that congressional experts didn't bother to question. For example, at the same time the federal government was paying enormous sums to maintain and expand an irrigation system in California's Imperial Valley, it was paying farmers on fertile nonirrigated lands enormous sums not to grow. Then, having paid to irrigate, the government paid the Imperial Valley's farmers not to grow cotton, wheat, and other crops on that land.

Despite the considerable power of the secretary of agriculture, the willingness of Butz's predecessor to use that power, the high cost of farm programs, and the professed concern about consumers, the members of the Senate Agriculture Committee unanimously believed that farm prices were too low. Each wanted Butz to use our nation's farm policy to raise prices, realizing, of course, that higher farm prices brought higher food prices.

Butz fulfilled half the committee's wishes. As secretary he raised prices to levels the press routinely described as "astronomical." He did it by destroying the system of programs that had been our nation's farm policy since 1933. By the time he left office, the handful of congressional experts together with the secretary of agriculture were no longer able to establish American agricultural policy. Their power had been taken away.

---

1. In 1972 the government did not buy and store sugar. Even though there was a world surplus, the other techniques for keeping prices high were considered sufficient.

Chapter Three

The Department of Agriculture Is Not a Department of Agriculture

I love every movement
There's nothing I would change
She doesn't need improvement
She's much too nice to rearrange.
—"Poetry in Motion"
by Kaufman and Anthony

R ichard Nixon proposed abolishing the Department of Agriculture less than a year before he nominated Earl Butz as its secretary. In a message to Congress on March 25, 1971 President Nixon said, "The Department of Agriculture was . . . added in the nineteenth century, at a time when the overwhelming majority of our people were directly affected by the tremendous expansion of agricultural enterprise. . . . It has sometimes been argued that certain interest groups need a department to act as their special representative within the Government. In my view, such an arrangement serves the best interest of neither the special group nor the general public. Little is gained and much can be lost, for example, by treating our farmers . . . as if they are independent participants in our economic life. Their problems cannot be adequately treated in isolation; their well-being is intimately related to the way our entire economy functions." The USDA's agricultural programs were to be transferred to an agency in a proposed Economic Development Department.

The plan, which would have reorganized most federal cabinet departments, soon ran into political trouble and was quietly neglected. Butz later said that he had agreed to take the job only if Nixon scrapped his idea to abolish the USDA. "That was a condition of my coming," Butz said. Butz's predecessor had found himself in the awkward position of testifying to abolish his own department, which helped neither the secretary's nor the department's stature.

According to the *United States Government Manual*, "The Department of Agriculture (USDA) serves all Americans daily. It works to improve and maintain farm income and to develop and expand markets abroad for agricultural products. The Department helps to curb and cure poverty, hunger, and malnutrition. It works to enhance the environment and to maintain our production capacity by helping landowners protect the soil, water, forests, and other natural resources. Rural development, credit, and conservation programs are key resources for carrying out national growth policies. USDA research findings directly or indirectly benefit all Americans. The Department, through inspection and grading services, safeguards and assures standards of quality in the daily food supply."

In 1972 Agriculture was the fourth largest department in the federal government, even though only 4.6 percent of the American people lived and worked on farms. During one appropriations battle, a Michigan representative half-jokingly offered an amendment prohibiting USDA from hiring more employees than there were farmers. The amendment was defeated. Only Treasury, Defense, and HEW had more employees.[1] Agriculture was larger than such departments as State, Justice, Commerce, Labor, Interior, and Housing and Urban Development.

Most of the Agriculture Department's budget was

devoted to issues other than agriculture, however. It was primarily a welfare agency. In 1975, when USDA spent $1.7 billion for agricultural research and price supports for farmers, the food-stamp program alone cost $4.4 billion and about two-thirds of USDA's budget supplemented income for the nation's poor. By 1977 the Senate Agriculture Committee expressed concern that USDA did not have the money to devote adequate attention to farm issues. "It is evident," the committee noted, "that income security programs . . . are taking a larger share of the Department's budget. However, the real problem is not the increase in income security programs. The basic problem is lack of support for the agriculture function."[2]

Most USDA employees did not work on farm issues. In 1972 the largest single agency in the department was the Forest Service with nearly 20,493 employees, put in Agriculture by Teddy Roosevelt because he believed that Interior was insensitive to conservation.

Of the USDA's 82,511 full-time employees, most worked in cities. When Butz served as secretary, he complained that 23,000 USDA employees had what he called "police power." They inspected chickens and hot dogs, closing down unsanitary food-processing plants. They investigated food-stamp fraud, prevented American tourists from bringing Polish sausages into the U.S., and quarantined race horses.

Only a small percentage of the department's personnel saw farmers on a regular basis. The founder of the Agricultural Extension Service was commemorated by a memorial arch across Independence Avenue, but in 1972 the service had only 240 federal staff, including secretaries, teaching farmers about the latest agricultural research. In 1975 Ed Jones, a Democratic representative from Tennessee, complained that there were too few rural offices. "Soon the Department's only presence in farm areas will be a computer terminal."

The Department had lost its constituency of farmers by attrition, had neglected its services to the remainder, and had redefined its function to represent farmers' interests while simultaneously expending large sums to maintain a large bureaucracy, one of whose functions was to regulate the very interests it promoted.

The result was a department with fundamental conflict-of-interest problems. For example it promoted the sale of chickens that it inspected for purity. The USDA was supposed to help lumber companies increase sales while protecting the national forests, whose trees it permitted the companies to cut down. It promoted exporters' sales of grain while licensing the inspection of the same grain.

Periodically the conflicts became so overwhelming that remedial action was needed. In 1970 the USDA encouraged farmers to use pesticides and also enforced safeguards related to pesticides, and its inefficiency at regulating use was widely acknowledged. This function was transferred to the newly created Environmental Protection Agency. After the 1972 Soviet wheat deal, widespread abuses on USDA-regulated commodity exchanges prompted the creation of an independent agency to regulate the exchanges. Congress decided that the USDA was too close to the grain trade to do an impartial job. A similar agency was proposed to inspect grain when a scandal developed in 1975. Congress eventually created a special inspection agency within the USDA and provided special safeguards to protect its independence.

Despite these demonstrated conflicts in purpose, USDA officials continued to define the department, in the words of one assistant secretary, as "a spokesman for the American farm community." The interests of the "farm community," however, often differed from the interests of consumers and the poor, other constituencies the USDA was also obliged to serve. Organizationally the department made little at tempt to prevent its legal obligations to one constituency from improperly affecting its obligations to another, so it continued to operate at cross purposes with itself.

Many of its functions were also duplicated by other departments. For example, it was only one of several agencies protecting the purity of food. Agriculture inspected meat, eggs, and poultry; Commerce inspected tuna fish; and HEW's Food and Drug Administration made sure that there weren't contaminants such as rodent pellets and dead insects in various packaged food products. In some years Agriculture's Rural Housing Administration built more homes than the Department of Housing and Urban Development. The USDA shared decision-making powers on agricultural policy issues with such departments as Commerce and State. In fact by 1976 a congressional study found that the USDA was only one of 22 separate agencies making agricultural policy.

Despite this confusion of purpose compounded by diffusion of function, by the time Earl Butz took office, Agriculture had firmly established its reputation for boredom and obscurity. The agency produced reports on feedgrain sales to Poland, researched diseases in swine, and developed and refined corn hybrids. Every Washington bureaucracy was criticized for the esoteric quality of its expertise, but the USDA's irrelevance to most Americans' daily lives appeared especially pronounced. Later when *The Washington Star* needed a dull, stereotyped workplace for its newspaper soap opera, it created a fictional Chicken and Egg Division in the USDA.

Although its work may have been useful, until Butz became secretary, the Department of Agriculture was rarely consulted on important decisions. For decades the secretary of agriculture was routinely ignored by the president, most members of Congress, and the majority of the cabinet, and this occurred so frequently that the secretary was often not even present when the president made major agricultural policy decisions.

The department had gradually evolved to its lowly status. In 1862, when most of the nation's people lived and worked on farms, Abraham Lincoln created the Department of Agriculture. It had 10 employees. Creating the department was part of a package; in the same year Lincoln signed a homestead bill giving 160 free acres to anyone settling the frontier, a land-grant-college act to make sure farmers could learn how to use their land well, and a transcontinental railroad act to ensure, among other things, that farmers settling the frontier would have a means of getting their crops to market.

The role of the department was primarily informational. It issued statistics and data on crops, crop conditions, and different varieties of plants. It also conducted research on such problems as animal and plant diseases to help farmers who had responded to the government-wide effort to settle the frontier.

When the transcontinental railroad was completed, the railroad companies were especially eager to encourage homesteaders, who would become steady customers. They mounted a major publicity campaign to dispel rumors that the West was a huge desert and to convince families to move to little-known territories.

In 1878 the Burlington and Missouri River Railroad advertised cheap and free land in southern Iowa and southeastern Nebraska. One observer reported, "I have never, before coming here, taken much stock in the stories of wonderfully cheap homes in the West, but I find people here . . . living almost in affluence on their prairie home, who I know left New York State only a few years ago with next to nothing."

Soon the opportunity was gone for people without land or money to become wealthy by farming the frontier. In

1890 historian Frederick Jackson Turner discovered the frontier was gone. Reading the census returns for that year, he wrote, "This marks the closing of a great historical movement. Up to our own day American history has been in a large degree the history of the colonization of the Great West. The existence of an area of free land, . . . and the advance of the American settlement westward, explain American development."

Before the nineteenth century was over, the cause of the small farmer in America was probably dead. Many people who had been lured into settling the frontier by free land from the government or the railroads had mortgaged their farms to pay for expensive machinery. (McCormick had produced reapers on a large scale in its Chicago factory since 1847.) With technology making crops plentiful and speculators keeping prices artificially low, thousand-acre farms were developed to produce large enough crops to meet production costs. By 1889 wheat farmers received 30 percent less income than in 1881, even though the crop was 25 percent larger. Populists in Nebraska sang the ditty: "So it goes, the same old story, with the farmer as a goat;/He can only pay his taxes and the interest on his note./Oh, it's fun to be a farmer and to till the dusty soil,/But the guys who farm the farmers are the ones who get the spoil."

The government was called upon increasingly to protect farmers against abuse of power, to keep the nation's food supply from falling into the hands of a few powerful people, and to provide the family farmer with the latest developments in agriculture. As the populist agrarian movement developed, it was influential in passing laws that established protective tariffs, controlled trusts, and regulated railroads and water rights.

The movement also developed an eloquent political rhetoric that expressed the anguish of families squeezed off the land by economic forces they didn't understand and couldn't control. William Jennings Bryan's "Thou shall not crucify mankind on a cross of gold" speech was a proposal for solving farm problems. In his argument against the gold standard, he was suggesting that heavily mortgaged farmers be permitted to pay off their debts in silver, which was cheaper than gold. Like other people who came up with ready answers to difficult questions, Bryan was regarded as too simplistic and, eventually, as something of a buffoon. But his Nebraska rhetoric (which persuaded Hubert Humphrey's father to become a Democrat) and the clear predicament the bipartisan populist movement expressed created the political momentum for agricultural controls by the time FDR became president.

From 1900 to 1930 the farm population declined from 40 percent of the American people to 25 percent. In 1933 when Henry Wallace, FDR's controversial secretary of agriculture, took office, the USDA was still emphasizing education. Because farmers were too busy working their farms to attend land-grant colleges, the USDA sent out "extension" agents to teach the latest techniques in, for example, preventing swine disease and getting more ears of corn to the acre.

Farmers' economic problems had become so severe that the majority of farmers enthusiastically supported drastic action to prevent surpluses and raise prices, such as slaughtering baby pigs and destroying crops in the field. When Wallace instituted these actions, which on the surface seemed irrational, he had the necessary political support. The populist movement's expression of genuine grievances had finally convinced the government to take whatever action was necessary to save the family farm.

In 1933 agricultural policy was also social policy. Twenty-five percent of the American people lived and worked on farms, and as long as they stayed, they could prevent a small number of individuals and corporations from dominating the country's agricultural policy because they still produced most of the country's food. It was also social policy, because the government was not simply supporting their business, it was helping preserve their way of life. Had the policy succeeded, America would have a broader range of options today, both agriculturally and socially.

Instead there were mass migrations to the cities. Each year from 1940 to 1960 one million people left their farms. Urban areas became filled with unskilled laborers, many of whom were forced to go on welfare. The opportunity to live in the country and make an adequate income from farming had been closed off to all but a few people.

In 1972 other industrial countries, such as France and Switzerland, still devoted considerable resources to keeping a relatively large percentage of the population tilling small, often inefficient holdings. These governments had political support for farm policies that resulted in higher per capita food costs. Critics of American policy frequently pointed to these countries, arguing that the costs of subsidized farming were more than balanced by decreased welfare and social costs in urban areas. Whatever the merits of these arguments, a multibillion-dollar governmentally sponsored program that would break up large land holdings and repopulate farm communities in the United States was not politically or economically possible. Agriculture's large, capital-intensive, highly specialized operations had become an integral part of the American economy that could not be disassembled without dismantling the economy as a whole.

The clear distinction between agricultural and social policy was not made overnight. It evolved slowly as more people left their farms and as efforts to stop the migration became clumsy and inefficient.

The milk program certainly confused social policy with agricultural policy. In 1974, there were 83,699 dairy farmers in Wisconsin, upper New York, and other rural areas who would be gone in another generation because they were 55 years of age or older. Their typical farm was worth about

$137,000, and they earned about $8,000 a year—less than a salaried worker earned at a large dairy. Because cows have to be milked twice a day, many of these farmers had not been off the farm for more than a day or two at a time in more than ten years. Their children didn't want to live that life and couldn't afford to anyway.

The USDA used the Depression-born farm program to subsidize these farmers. Since they were too old to enter another business, subsidizing them was preferable to making them go on welfare, and their continued work was an historical asset as an example of the way farming used to be. But it would have been cheaper, and in some cases more humane, to mail them an annual income check.

Instead the USDA pretended that keeping them in business was agricultural policy. Because they produced only a small percentage of the country's milk products, the USDA's price supports—which raised the price of all milk—gave them an inadequate income while unnecessarily subsidizing large dairies. The program also imposed trade barriers on dairy products, antagonizing foreign customers and giving them cause to restrain our exports. Then the USDA, under the pretense of providing nutritional supplements to the poor, used school-lunch and other programs to dump surplus dairy products. For example milk was distributed to low-income black and Asian children, even though the USDA knew that many of them were allergic to milk because of a little-understood racial characteristic and became sick when they drank it. In the end the USDA's confusion of social policy with agricultural policy had made a mockery of both while causing the public to pay significantly higher prices for milk.

Earl Butz realized that the Department of Agriculture was not an effective place to be if he wanted to get something done. Given the dynamics of power in Washington, he realized that doing something would be a herculean task, especially with an old-line government agency as entrenched and multipurposed as Agriculture. But he was interested in doing nothing, or more precisely in having the Agriculture Department do as little as possible to determine the country's farm policy.

He understood that farming had become big business and that it could pay for itself. He believed populist rhetoric was no longer effective. He was convinced that, if given the choice, the public would no longer support programs that:

- paid farmers not to grow;
- prohibited farmers from growing what they wanted because their fathers or grandfathers did not receive wheat, corn, or other allotments; and
- charged foreign consumers less for American products than we were paying.

Butz created a choice by putting the agricultural economy in turmoil, by destroying the programs that were the life's blood of the agency he had sworn to uphold. As secretary of agriculture, he had control over the price and supply of our country's basic food products. Although his control was not total, for about 40 years other secretaries had helped keep prices and supplies of agricultural commodities relatively stable. If he could introduce instability where there had once been stability, then he could change the country's agricultural policy. All he had to do was create a food shortage.

---

1. In 1980 the Department of Health, Education and Welfare (HEW) changed its name to Health and Human Services (HHS) when an independent Department of Education was established.

2. During the 1970s, the purpose of food-stamps and other nutritional feeding programs had changed. Originally created as a method of dumping surplus commodities, they had become instead primarily a method for supplementing income. When Butz first began referring

to these programs as welfare, he aroused controversy, especially among liberals who opposed Butz's efforts to transfer them to the Department of Health, Education and Welfare where they would be more vulnerable to budget cuts. During the 1970s, farm interests attacked feeding programs at a time when surpluses had disappeared and the programs no longer served to raise farm income. By the Carter Administration, liberals and conservatives alike viewed the programs primarily as income support despite the return of agricultural surpluses.

Chapter Four

Creating a Food Shortage

> "You amuse me because we have conversed so often
> and so intelligently about the stream of history. We have
> agreed that no man can change events, and yet here
> you have been to-night, trying to change them. . . ."
>
> He sipped at his tea again; then he drew a fan
> from behind his neckband, a gold and black fan like
> the lacquer of the chairs, and waved it slowly in
> front of him. I was obliged to admit that his words
> were true, that I was interfering instead of watching
> the world go by: yet there seemed no way out of it
> now that I had begun.
>
> — *Thank You, Mr. Moto*
> by John Marquand

It may be difficult to create a food shortage when there isn't one. Earl Butz didn't have that problem, however. All he had to do was create a food shortage when there was one.

In 1972 world food production was no longer keeping up with population, which was growing at the rate of 80 million people a year, or the total population of the U.S. every 30 months. World grain production fell by 35 million metric tons.[1] Two years of bad weather worldwide had emptied world grain reserves. The U.S. was the only country with any grain in storage, and if that were depleted, the world's only defense against starvation would be the crops already in the ground. There was drought in India, China, Australia, Russia, and West Africa. Simultaneously the world's fish catch unexpectedly began shrinking, further reducing grain supplies because fish is a principal ingredient in livestock feed.

There were, in fact, two different kinds of food shortages in the world. One concerned survival, the other—for want of a better word—comfort. While some countries were starving, others were spending money to make their diets more interesting by doing what USDA officials called "upgrading the quality of the diet," or eating more hamburger, chicken, steak, and processed foods.

The two shortages reflected different patterns of grain consumption. In China, for example, the average person consumed 450 pounds of grain annually, 350 of them as rice or some cereal product. The other 100 pounds were fed to livestock to produce an occasional meal containing chicken or pork. At the same time the average American consumed more than 2000 pounds of grain annually but 90 percent of it was used to feed livestock.

Some countries were changing their patterns. In late 1971 the Soviets announced an ambitious five-year plan to increase the average worker's consumption of meat and other animal products by 25 percent. The per capita income of Japan, Korea, West Germany, and several Arab countries increased, and so did their willingness to import American grain to upgrade their diet.

Thus while nutritionists were suggesting that a diet based on grain was healthier than one based on animal products, an increasing percentage of the world's population was demanding the latter. World meat consumption increased during a period of agricultural shortfalls, so two grain-based shortages were created, one of grain for survival and one of meat and other animal products.

But observers in the United States had difficulty believing either that the world food shortage was real or that it had any relevance to this country. After all, the government was keeping prices high and increasing surpluses. The

USDA paid farmers not to grow crops on 38 million acres, 14 million of them wheat land. It paid $642 million a year to store surpluses. Farmers were selling their grain at incredibly low prices, $1.54 a bushel for wheat and $1.04 for corn. Because market prices were so low, for each bushel of wheat selling for $1.54, the USDA gave the farmer a 25-cent subsidy to cover production costs. Congressional farm leaders from both parties condemned these subsidies as too low. Even though America dominated the world's grain trade with more than a 50-percent market share, the government had little confidence in this country's ability to sell in world markets. So foreign buyers got a 23-cent discount on every bushel of wheat and 10 cents on corn. That is, if a German bread manufacturing company agreed to purchase wheat in Kansas City for $1.54 a bushel, the company paid only $1.31, and the farmer got a USDA check for 23 cents. An American bread manufacturer, on the other hand, had to pay the full $1.54.

Paradoxically the traditional methods used to keep prices high actually kept prices low by isolating American agriculture from world conditions. Prices in the grain markets at Chicago, Kansas City, and Minneapolis remained low because buyers believed that there was little demand for grain, and the government's policies supported this belief. Grain could not be in short supply, buyers reasoned, if the government was willing to store grain, to pay farmers not to grow, to subsidize prices, and to subsidize exports. The sellers reasoned that if they asked too much for their grain and prices went up, then the government would flood the market with surpluses and open up additional farmland for production. That in turn would send prices even lower than they were already.

Earl Butz was fortunate because his first full year in office coincided with the election year during which, as subsequent events made perfectly clear, incumbent Richard Nixon was trying not to leave anything to chance. The political climate provided Butz with considerable latitude as long as he produced results.

One desired result was raising farm income. Although farmers were less than 5 percent of the population, their vote was considered significant. In 1968, for example, Nixon was elected with a popular margin of less than 1 percentage point; had farmers voted against him, he would have lost. Unlike other voting blocks, farmers have high turnout records. They traditionally vote Republican, but this tradition was at risk because farmers blame low prices on the administration in power. Therefore good campaign strategy demanded improved farm income. Grain farmers were the largest and most influential segment of the farm community, and regardless of political or economic perspective, the country's agricultural experts agreed that something had to be done somehow to raise grain prices.

Butz's first move was to use the traditional price-raising measures he had condemned. In January 1972 he announced that he would flood the farm belt with a record $4 billion in payments and would withhold additional land from production. Farmers would be paid not to grow crops on more than 62 million acres, as opposed to 38 million the year before. This meant that America was deliberately making the world grain shortage even worse by planting less.

In theory, as world crops were being wiped out by bad weather and world demand was increasing, the market price of wheat, corn, and soybeans would have to go up, and when prices went up, so would farm income. There was, however, the risk that withholding still more land from production would further isolate the marketplace from world conditions and paradoxically continue to lower prices.

Butz dealt with that problem by setting into motion a series of events that led to a secret grain deal with the Soviets, the largest agricultural sale in world history. Buyers on U.S. commodity markets suddenly discovered that the only grain in storage in the world was unexpectedly gone at the same time that current crops were significantly smaller.

Less than a year after Butz took office, the price of wheat went from $1.54 a bushel to $2.26, corn went from $1.04 to $1.35, and all grain prices climbed sharply and continually. Wheat prices hit 25-year highs. Before the November election, it was already clear that annual net farm income was going to be the highest in history. Prices were so high that for most programs the Agriculture Department no longer needed to help farmers pay production costs. The government stopped discounting the sale of grain abroad. Because the Soviets had emptied our storage bins, the Agriculture Department was no longer paying storage costs on grain, and it began selling off the bins. Many farmers, attracted by high prices, wanted to plant more and convinced the government to curtail programs paying them not to grow. Not only had the Nixon administration managed to increase farm income, it also significantly reduced the costs of farm programs.

There was a considerable lag time until high farm prices passed through the system to the retail level and made a significant impact on the householder's food budget. By then the election was over. Less than a year later people paid considerably more to feed their families; the American food bill jumped from an annual $141 billion in 1971 to $226 billion in 1976. The world food shortage had hit this country.

Meanwhile the Soviet sales were sufficiently timely that they helped improve the Commerce Department's balance-of-trade figures (showing whether the country is buying more goods than it is selling). These figures are one indicator of how well the economy is doing. In 1972 the economy was not doing well; there was both high unemployment and high inflation. So it helped Richard Nixon politically to show before the election that he had reduced the deficit, giving the impression that he was beginning to get the economy under control. Indeed, few voters associated the improvement in the Commerce Department figures with agriculture, and few agriculture experts believed that grain exports would become a significant factor in international trade. In Fiscal Year 1972 America's total agricultural exports were worth only $6.7 billion. The following year they were worth $11.9 billion. By 1974 farm exports rose to $20.4 billion and created a U.S. trade surplus even though the price of imported petroleum had quadrupled.

Back in April 1972, when it was trying to sell grain to the Soviets, the U.S. started bombing and mining Haiphong Harbor in Vietnam, where the Soviets had ships at anchor. *The New York Times* called Nixon's bombing a "deliberate confrontation" with the Soviets. In the same month Pravda, the Soviet newspaper, announced that because of extensive crop damage the Russian government had instituted a crash program to provide its people adequate food supplies. So while Americans mined and bombed North Vietnam to prevent Soviet foods from entering, the Soviet Union was secretly negotiating to buy 19 million metric tons of U.S. grain. The Soviets got what they wanted, cheap. Richard Nixon got away with taking a hard line against the Soviets without escalating Vietnam into a world war, which helped him at the polls.[2]

---

1. Compared to a total American wheat crop of 42 million metric tons.

2. It is perhaps an interesting footnote that during the Presidential campaign of 1984, when Ronald Reagan's critics said that U.S.-Soviet relations were at an historic low, the Soviets went on a massive buying spree. From June 1984 until the November election, the Soviets purchased 15.2 million metric tons of U.S. wheat and corn.

Chapter Five

The Russian Grain Deal

"Bah. Nothing is obvious in itself. Obviousness is subjective. Three pursuers learn that a fugitive boarded a train for Philadelphia. To the first pursuer it's obvious that the fugitive has gone to Philadelphia. To the second pursuer it's obvious that he left the train at Newark and has gone somewhere else. To the third pursuer, who knows how clever the fugitive is, it's obvious that he didn't leave the train at Newark, because that would be too obvious, but stayed on it and went to Philadelphia. Subtlety chases the obvious up a never-ending spiral and never quite catches it."
— Nero Wolfe in Rex Stout's
The Silent Speaker

After the Russian wheat deal was over, Congress tried to figure out what had happened. The House Subcommittee on Livestock and Grain called in the secretary of agriculture for questions. Representative John R. Rarick of Louisiana observed, "As a farmboy, I can remember my dear old Hoosier grandmother telling me to watch out for some American businessmen, they will trade with the Devil if they can make a profit." Earl Butz responded, "If he has dollars."

Many reacted to the sale as if America had in fact traded with the devil, and they blamed the Soviet wheat deal for such subsequent events as the sudden rise in retail food prices, famine in Asia, Africa, and Latin America, and the Nixon administration's cutbacks in "Food for Peace" and food-stamps. One populist group called it "The Great Grain Robbery." There is considerable literature describing how terrible it was.

This is what happened. When the Soviets had massive crop failures in 1972, they could have abandoned their five-year plan to increase consumption of meat and other animal products. Although the crop failures were later described as disastrous, they were only disastrous from the perspective of the plan, which had begun in late 1971 when Russia purchased high-quality breeding stock from the U.S. and Canada. The Soviets would not have needed to import grain in massive quantities if they had been willing to slaughter off their breeding stock and their growing livestock industry. Most observers in the U.S. and the rest of the world assumed they would abandon the plan, so rumors of Soviet crop failures had little effect on grain prices.

The Soviet leadership, however, was reluctant to renege on its promise to add more meat to the bland Russian diet of bread, potatoes, and other starches. They were concerned by food riots that had occurred and did not want to add to domestic discontent. They had also made a major investment in expensive breeding stock. They were reluctant to lose both the initial investment and the time it takes to produce livestock ready for slaughter—as much as a year for hogs and two years for steers. When they looked at the world market, they saw the opportunity to buy cheap grain.

In the summer of 1972 the Soviets bought 10 million metric tons of grain from the rest of the world and 19 million from the U.S. The U.S. sale, which earned an estimated $1.1 billion, included 12 million metric tons of wheat, 6 million of corn and other feedgrains, and 1 million of soybeans.[1] Because the American wheat was high quality, the Soviets could feed their low-quality wheat to livestock and use American wheat for making bread. Although it was popularly called a "wheat deal," "meat deal" is a more accurate description.

The United States had assured the Soviets back in 1971, when they purchased American breeding stock, that it would supply the Soviets with all the grain they needed. The Soviets, however, did not want this country or the rest of the world to know how massive their needs were or how much their economic plans depended on the sales. Nevertheless, because so much was at stake, they needed to be reassured in advance that the U.S. government would not unexpectedly interfere with the transaction. The long-term adversarial relationship between the two countries had resulted in legislation giving the president authority to prevent any sales.

Not only did President Nixon, Secretary Butz, and other officials provide the necessary reassurances, the Agriculture Department agreed to provide the Soviets $750 million in low-interest loans to buy the grain. President Nixon also lifted the usual requirement that 50 percent of the grain be carried on U.S. flag ships; transportation on them was more expensive than on ships of other nations, and they were in short supply because of the Vietnam War. Nixon made the Soviets' transportation arrangements cheaper and easier.

The U.S. government owned much of the grain for sale because the Department of Agriculture's Commodity Credit Corporation had bought farmers' wheat, corn, and other feedgrains, which it was paying $642 million a year to store. The Agriculture Department could have sold the grain directly to the Soviets. Instead, after negotiating with the Soviets, the government decided to sell all its grain in the marketplace. Private corporations bought it, and they in turn negotiated sales agreements with the Soviets.

Throughout the long process of negotiations and sales, the Soviets coordinated all the details through one central government buying agency, Exportkhelb. The American sellers, on the other hand, were haphazardly represented by the departments of Agriculture, Commerce, Transportation, and State, in addition to six multinational grain-trading companies and other governmental and private interests.

The U.S. government could have coordinated the massive sale and prevented the chaotic process whereby several sellers, relying on incomplete and inaccurate information, competed among themselves to give the Russians extremely low prices. The Department of Agriculture, the Central Intelligence Agency, and others provided reports on the Soviet crop, underestimating the shortfalls by tens of millions of bushels. At the minimum the U.S. government might have used its leverage to require the Soviets to provide reliable information on the extent of their crop failures.

Instead the government had so removed itself from the process that months after the transactions occurred, the Agriculture Department did not know whether the deal had actually taken place nor how much the Soviets had purchased. The Agriculture Department even lifted the requirement that grain-trading companies report on their export sales.

Secretary Butz later testified that he first learned that the Russians had bought American grain two months after the sales had taken place. In summer 1972, after the Soviets had already purchased 400 million bushels of wheat, an Agriculture Department publication stated, "There are indications that Soviet wheat purchases could easily exceed ... 65 million bushels."

The Agriculture Department was also criticized because it had close ties to the grain industry and because officials responsible for establishing government policy resigned to take high-paying positions in the grain companies. For example early in 1972 Assistant Secretary of Agriculture for International Affairs Clarence Palmby led the U.S. negotiating team in Moscow that decided to let the private companies rather than the USDA sell the grain. Palmby, who earned less than $40,000 a year, resigned his position at the USDA and went to work at $60,000 plus bonuses as vice president of the Continental Grain Company, which made the largest single sale of U.S. grain to the Soviets.

The Soviet Union bought America's grain from six multinational grain-trading companies: Cargill, Cook, Continental, Dreyfus, Garnac, and Bunge. Two of the six were categorized as "American companies," which meant they maintained corporate headquarters in the U.S. But only one, Cook Industries of Memphis, was publicly owned. Cook was therefore the only company required to disclose information to the Securities and Exchange Commission. The five privately owned companies kept secret basic information about their activities, organizational structure, and ownership. Later when the General Accounting Office did a report on the Russian deal, one company refused to supply information to the congressional investigators.

Little was known about the multinational grain trade not only by the general public, but also by people working on agricultural policy issues. For example in September 1972 Representative Frank Denholm of South Dakota asked USDA officials questions about collaboration between the Agriculture Department and the grain companies and specifically about Clifford Pulvermacher, who had retired as general sales manager for the USDA. The day before Bunge sold the Soviets 600,000 metric tons of wheat, Pulvermacher, who had gone to Moscow as part of the government's negotiating team, went to work for Bunge as head of its Washington office.

When asked where Pulvermacher was currently working, a USDA official testified that he wasn't sure, but "There was some suggestion that he is Washington representative of the Bunge Corp." Denholm asked, "Who is Bunge?" The incredulous USDA official said, "That is an interna tional trading company, and there is probably not a person in this room who doesn't know it." The congressman said, "I am just a farm boy. I am not familiar with international grain cartels." The official, still incredulous, said, "You don't know Bunge?" Representative Denholm said, "I have never sold my grain and wheat to any foreign exporter or international grain cartel."

What made that exchange so incredible was that a congressman serving on the Agriculture Committee really did not know "who" Bunge was. It would be equivalent to a congressman from Detroit, serving on a committee concerned with the automobile industry, who had never heard of the Ford Motor Company. Yet because American agriultural policy had been so consistently isolationist, members of congressional agriculture committees and even officials at the USDA who had spent their lives on issues such as parity, farm subsidies, and import quotas, were familiar neither with how the business of agriculture worked, nor with the principal players. Representative Denholm and his farmer constituents in South Dakota had no way of knowing whether they had sold their grain to Bunge or any other "international grain cartel." Farmers frequently did not know who was actually buying their products.

Although a grain-trading company could own or lease farmland, factories, railroad cars, grain elevators, or other businesses, its primary concern was to buy and sell grain at a profit. The company was not interested in the grain itself, but acted as an intermediary, purchasing grain from the farmer or whoever had it and delivering it to the buyer. When large quantities were involved and the buyers were far from where the grain was grown, this role was essential. Obtaining the grain and shipping it to a specified place at a specified time required considerable organization. Contracts with a trading company, for example, could require delivery of corn to New Orleans in two months, soybeans to London in six months, or wheat to Odessa in a year. In return for its service the company figured its fee, often as little as a penny or two a bushel, into the selling price. The low rate was profitable because of the enormous volume involved. In 1975 the six major companies controlled more than 90 percent of an $11-billion-a-year grain-export business.

Two characteristics of the business that figured into the Russian deal are first, because competition was intense, no company wanted the others to know what it was doing. For example none wanted the others to know its selling price for wheat, for fear a competitor would then go to the buyer and offer to sell for less.

Second, a company generally did not have the grain when it signed a sales contract. Sales contracts provided delivery at a future time and place, and a company generally went out and bought the grain only after it had a contract. No company wanted the marketplace to know how much it had contracted to sell, however, because nothing raises prices faster than news that someone has to buy regardless of price. So each company operated in secret to avoid the disastrous situation of being obliged to buy grain at prices higher than its contracts to sell would bring in.

The Russians used the trade's inherent secrecy to their advantage. On September 13, 1972, the president of the Bunge Corporation described the sales to the House Agriculture Committee:

"We were first in telephone contact with Exportkhelb representatives in late June while they were in Washington, and we tried to set up a meeting to determine their interest. On July 7 we visited them, at their request, in their hotel suite at the New York Hilton Hotel for our first business discussion. We asked them about their potential grain requirements, and, based on their known desire to increase their meat and protein intake, we expected them to be interested in corn, barley, or soybeans. They denied interest in these commodities and to our surprise requested an offer for wheat. On Monday, July 10, we offered 600,000 tons of hard red winter wheat but failed to do the business, and we were told that our price was too high. In late July, with no knowledge of USSR total requirements, we resumed negotiations and on August 2 sold Exportkhelb 600,000 tons of hard red winter wheat. Despite later press reports making numerous and varied estimates, from which wheat purchased seemed to have reached 10/12 million tons, we do not know to this day the actual USSR purchases or requirements. . . . We further would like to add that Bunge Corporation, even at this time, does not know what the financial outcome of our wheat sale to the USSR will be, since a large part of the physical wheat must still be purchased and all of the wheat has still to be shipped."

The president of the Continental Grain Company rented a yacht so that he and the chief of Exportkhelb could talk. The president of Cook Industries said that he and his competitors were frantically trying to meet the Russians to make a deal. They flew to Moscow, Washington, and New York. The Russians were playing hard to get.

It was the Russians, rather than the American businesspeople, who controlled the situation. The Russians appeared in no hurry to buy, but the Americans were in a great hurry to sell. Exportkhelb delayed requests for meetings, asked the eager salesmen to meet them on short notice in hotel suites, refused early bids, and tantalized companies with news of meetings with competitors. Because each of the signed contracts was a secret, the companies that sold the grain and even the U.S. government did not know the total amount the Russians had bought until months afterward. Later when the General Accounting Office looked at the books, one grain company reported that it had lost an average of 1.9 cents a bushel on the deal.

The Department of Agriculture even paid an export subsidy on the grain the Soviets bought. Later Congress learned that the USDA had simply forgotten to lift that device when it dumped grain surpluses on the world. The trading companies, however, did not forget. When they signed contracts with the Soviets, the companies took into account the $300 million in subsidies they would receive, so they charged the Russians discount prices. The Soviets bought, at less than $1.35 a bushel, wheat that in less than a year was selling for more than $4.00. But to this day only the Soviets know exactly how much they paid for their grain.

Planning, coordination, and secrecy provided the Soviet Union with several other advantages. Early in 1972, well before the summer grain deal, Exportkhelb made advanced purchases of space on cargo ships, using the London-based world market. Ship owners had no way of knowing that by summer they would be hauling 29 million metric tons of grain to the Soviet Union, so they sold the space at low prices. That summer, when the world's merchants tried to ship their goods, they found there was little space available, and it was expensive. Not only had the Soviets obtained favorable transportation rates, but they had deliberately overbooked. They then subcontracted the additional cargo space at high prices, and their profits were large enough to pay for transporting all their foreign grain purchases. Later American observers learned to use the London cargo market as a way of forecasting Soviet grain purchases. In 1975, for example, a Commodity News Service report on this activity alerted the U.S. government to another major Soviet grain deal.

Nor did the Americans pay attention to activity on gold exchanges. The Soviets, who were the second largest gold producers in the world, had to sell their gold to raise the foreign currencies, primarily dollars, needed for purchases in world markets. Prudence required that the Soviets sell their gold gradually to avoid dumping large quantities and lowering the price. Although firm evidence is difficult to obtain, the Soviets appeared to have profited on gold exchanges. They certainly profited from devaluation of the American dollar, which made buying American grain cheaper. There were also rumors, difficult to prove but perhaps true, of other Soviet profits. For example the Russians may have speculated on wheat futures at the Chicago Board of Trade. Congressional investigators even looked into stories that the Soviets had bought more American grain than needed and resold it at higher prices to others, including American customers.

America's transportation and food-production systems were not prepared for the massive Soviet grain purchases. Suddenly a quarter of the wheat crop was moving to Russia. America's decaying railroads were loaded with grain hoppers bound for ports where the Soviets had secured priority treatment. Farmers couldn't get their grain to market because railway cars and grain-elevator space were taken. Throughout rural America grain piled up in the streets. Domestic consumers, who needed grain for food products and feed, unexpectedly discovered that their warehouses were empty, and the transportation system was clogged with Russian-bound goods. Bakers worried that high-protein wheat needed to bake bread was in short supply. As it turned out there was enough, but these and other worries helped to raise prices precipitously. The General Accounting Office later estimated that Russian grain purchases in the summer of 1972 directly cost Americans about $1 billion extra on their food bill.

It was like the antique-dealer stories about a person eager to rid the living room of an old chair. Only after he sold it for a pittance did he realize it was worth a fortune. Americans suddenly discovered that they wished they hadn't sold the grain after all — at least not at bargain prices. The food system had been used to surpluses that were suddenly gone. On second thought, many expert witnesses told several congressional committees, perhaps that surplus grain hadn't really been a nuisance after all. Perhaps the grain had actually been a reserve against world hunger.

Earl Butz was then ready to destroy America's farm policy.

----

1. Technically soybeans are not a grain. Because they are often used the same way, however, some agricultural experts put them in the same category as grain, especially during nontechnical discussions. The author, intending to make the reader's task as nontechnical as possible, will henceforth refer to soybeans as a grain.

Chapter Six

Fear of Famine and Plenty

I am by nature an optimist. I think that if you can pretend that everything is going to be all right, and go ahead doing things just as if you didn't have to worry, your troubles may go away. Mostly they don't go away, I know, and then you're in a worse mess than ever. But I'm used to messes, and when you're desperate what else is there to do but pretend?
                                                    —*Dirty Story*
                                                    by Eric Ambler

In January 1973 the American consumer paid 20 percent more for food than a month earlier. By the end of the year the national cost of eating had increased by $18 billion.

In April angry consumers protested rising food prices by participating in a week-long boycott of meat. The boycott was organized by the Consumer Federation of America led by Carol Tucker Foreman, who later became President Carter's assistant secretary of agriculture for food and consumer service.

The boycott designed to lower prices helped raise them by disrupting the orderly marketing of a perishable commodity. Also, the boycott helped increase the economic pressures driving livestock producers out of business.

Although 1973 brought the highest farm income up to that point in American history, not all farmers shared in the windfall, which was entirely the result of high grain prices. Since there were more grain producers than other farmers, their increased revenues raised farm income in 1972 by 32.7 percent, compared to a total national income increase of 11.9 percent. Much of their profits, however — about two-thirds of the increase in food costs — came directly at the expense of farmers producing beef, poultry, eggs, and other animal products.

Farmers raising both grain and livestock realized they were losing money by feeding corn and soybeans to animals, especially since the annual average price of a bushel of corn shot up from $1.57 in 1972 to $2.55 in 1973. During 1973 soybean prices on the Chicago Board of Trade increased by 400 percent. Although beef and hog prices were rising, the increases were not nearly enough to pay rising production costs. Farmers had the option of selling their soybeans and corn at a profit using their high-priced grain as feed and, if current prices continued, losing more money feeding their livestock than the livestock was worth. Many gave up the livestock business suddenly.

From 1972 to 1976 farmers sold off their hogs and steers before they were fully mature, supplying the market with meat but drastically reducing future supplies. By 1975 there were fewer hogs than at any time since the 1930s, and the USDA said there would be 4 percent less milk, 16 percent less butter, and 13 percent less cheese than in 1974. In 1974 Senator Humphrey had observed, "Dairy cows on farms stayed at . . . the lowest level in almost 100 years." That year poultry production was down, there were fewer eggs, and the USDA noted, "The laying flock was . . . the lowest on record. . . . "

At the time it was difficult to know whether these declines resulted from uneconomical operators going out of business or were a real threat to the country's food supply. For example, declines in the number of dairy cattle were more than balanced by spectacular production increases. In 1935 the average dairy cow in New York State produced 5480 pounds of milk, by 1968, 9820 pounds of milk, and by 1985 the predictions were 13,300 pounds per cow.

The meat boycott hit livestock producers when they were in the midst of what South Dakota's secretary of agriculture later called "the growing depression in our national livestock industry." The Consumer Federation of America had targeted meat because it is easier to boycott than soybeans and wheat and because consumers were enraged by the dramatic rise in meat prices. The success of the boycott established the consumer movement as a potent force that, for the first time, played a significant role in making the government's agricultural policy.

Ironically the consumer movement, especially the Consumer Federation of America, lobbied Congress to dismantle the same farm programs that Earl Butz opposed. Even though they were in effect allies in such efforts as lifting restrictions on planting wheat and corn, changing sugar policy, and encouraging rice production, Earl Butz and the consumer groups engaged in nonstop feuding. The consumer groups portrayed Butz as the villain responsible for delivering over the country's agricultural policy to agribusiness during the Russian grain deal as part of a plan to gouge the American consumer with high food prices. Butz, in turn, characterized consumer advocates as naive do-gooders incapable of understanding the sophisticated business of agriculture. He called them "phony consumer representatives" and said, "They don't speak for anybody. They're just a bunch of phony agitators out for 30 seconds on the nightly network news."

Back at Butz's 1971 confirmation hearings, Senator Henry Bellmon (a Republican from Oklahoma) had worried that Butz would not attract the public attention necessary to explain agricultural policy. "One thing that troubles me as a farmer and as a representative of a farm state, is that agriculture has not had a highly visible, articulate, dedicated spokesman at the national level." At the same occasion Senator Humphrey said, "The best thing we have had happen this morning is the fact . . . somebody is interested in agriculture down here in Washington, and we are getting some news. I know it is at the expense of Dr. Butz, but I have not read or heard anything about agriculture for so long in the public domain, in the printed word, in the electronic media. . . . "

Suddenly, because of the consequences of the Russian grain deal, agricultural policy received widespread attention from the press, from Congress, and from the public. Although as a result Secretary Butz was subjected to intense scrutiny over allegations that there were improprieties in the relationships between the USDA and grain traders as well as others, the attention also gave Butz the political support he needed for legislative victories. For the first time in decades a secretary of agriculture emerged as a major governmental policy-maker whose views were widely heard and discussed.

Butz, however, reacted to the intense publicity in a fiercely combative manner and attacked people who were newly interested in farm policy as "instant agriculture experts"; issued curt denunciations of people interested in feeding the country's poor and the world's hungry; and told embarrassingly crude and insensitive "jokes," often sounding like a combined partisan hack and country bumpkin. Although he had been a dean of agriculture at Purdue University and was one of only a handful of high-level public officials to have received a Ph.D., it became commonplace for journalists, members of Congress, consumer advocates, and others to question his intelligence publicly.

On June 27, 1973, President Nixon, afraid there would not be enough food for the American people, embargoed the export of soybeans. Only two weeks earlier he had told Congress that he lacked the legal authority to do so. After the Department of Agriculture compared crop reports with reports on foreign purchases, however, it found the U.S. had apparently sold four times the soybeans that it owned. At the same time heavy rains and flooding were damaging crops, and the administration worried there might not be enough grain.

Earl Butz's embargo statement said, "I want to make sure we will have adequate supplies of meat, milk, and eggs. . . . " As it turned out crops were better off than had been feared, and reports of foreign sales were inflated. But for the first time in this century Americans were confronted with the possibility that there might not be adequate supplies of food. The soybean embargo clarified the significance of the 1972 Russian grain deal. Suddenly and unexpectedly, agriculture had gone from surplus to shortage. While the agricultural economy increasingly depended on foreign sales, public officials, union leaders, the press, consumer groups, and others questioned whether America could afford to export its grain. In 1974 and again in 1975, President Ford imposed additional embargoes on grain sales.[1] As in 1973, these hastily imposed embargoes were of questionable legality and effectiveness and only emphasized how powerless the U.S. government was to control its own agricultural policy.

On August 10, 1973, President Nixon signed a major farm bill turning over control of agriculture from the government to the marketplace. The bill affected most of the cropland in the nation. For the first time in decades farmers who produced wheat, corn, and other commodities depended entirely on market prices for their income. Previous law subsidized farmers regardless of the market, but under the new law even government payments were linked to prices.

The new system made payments according to "target prices," established minimum prices; if the market dropped beneath them, an eligible farmer would receive a government payment. The first target prices were set low, virtually guaranteeing that for at least two years farmers would receive no payments, or in the unlikely event that they did, the effect on their income would be negligible. For example the law established a target price for wheat of $2.05 a bushel. If market prices fell to $2.00, a farmer would receive 5 cents per bushel from the USDA. When the bill passed wheat prices averaged $4.54, and in 1974 when the policy first took effect, the average was $4.59. Even if market prices plunged unexpectedly, with rising production costs few farmers could afford to produce wheat at the $2.05 target price. In addition, payments were limited to $20,000, so even minimal governmental support per bushel would be cut before it could help a farmer survive economic disaster.

The law also lifted acreage restrictions, making such New Deal concepts as allotments and parity obsolete or, at best, of limited value. Suddenly it no longer mattered if one's parent or grandparent had received allotments. Any farmer with the money and desire could plant as much as he or she wanted anywhere he or she wanted.

High market prices and the lifting of government restrictions attracted people new to the business of farming and caused all grain farmers to plant as much as possible. Suddenly tens of millions of acres the government had paid farmers not to plant were opened up for production. Although the new law, the Agriculture and Consumer Protection Act of 1973, was limited to four years, it exposed American agriculture to dramatic economic and political change and made regaining previous levels of governmental control impossible.

In keeping with the spirit of the times, the word "consumer" appeared in the title of a major farm bill. Representative Leonor Sullivan (a Democrat from Missouri) tried unsuccessfully to delete the words "consumer protection" from the title. He argued that this description should be applied only to legislation dealing with consumer issues in a "direct and straightforward manner."

In February 1973, when the Senate Agriculture Committee had begun its hearings on a new bill, neither the secretary of agriculture nor any of the department's officials bothered to testify. Earl Butz permitted a USDA official to tell Senate staff members informally that the Department of Agriculture did not plan to submit a farm bill to Congress. If Congress wanted one, it would have to write its own, and to avoid a veto the bill would have to be acceptable to Earl Butz.

Butz did not really need a farm bill. Since there was a food shortage, he could use his current authority to permit farmers to grow as much as they wanted. He and the rest of the administration generally were afraid that the Democratic Congress would pass an expensive bill with large price supports for farmers and continued growth in food stamps and social programs. Faced with that, they preferred no legislation at all.

Even Butz did not realize the extent of change in the farm economy following the Russian grain deal. Although he advocated a "free market" approach to agriculture, he did not believe it would be politically achievable, at least not so quickly. He was still willing to compromise slow progress toward his long-term objectives by allowing a three-year phase-out of direct subsidies to farmers, if he were given authority to withhold land from production. He believed that it was still politically necessary to cushion agriculture from potential price-lowering surpluses until the farm economy was ready for complete deregulation.

Senate Agriculture Committee Chair Herman Talmadge (a Democrat from Georgia) told his colleagues that "the pressures on us here today to do nothing—to let existing legislation expire and eliminate permanent legislation on the books—is extremely great." He observed, "The U.S. House of Representatives has just been redistricted in such a way that the vast majority of its membership is from large cities and their suburbs. Food prices are higher than they have been in some time and many consumers are angry. The major metropolitan daily newspapers have begun what appears to be a massive campaign on their editorial pages to end the farm program. The President of the United States indicated that he wants to get government off the farm. Farm income is higher than it has ever been." Talmadge lamented that "drafting new farm legislation this year comes at what is perhaps the poorest possible psychological and political moment."

Without a new bill both food stamps and the Food for Peace programs would end. Many urban and suburban members of Congress were already alarmed by the administration's cutbacks, impoundments, and threats of reducing social services, including lunches for middle-class school-children. They were willing to secure programs that affected their constituents directly, such as food stamps, by compromising farm programs such as price supports for wheat that didn't directly affect them.

Farmers and the groups representing them were sharply divided on what they wanted and how badly they needed new legislation to achieve their goals. Grain farmers worried that unless new laws were passed they would be limited by existing restrictions. They were willing to compromise considerably the long-term security government programs offered as long as nothing prevented their benefiting from current high prices and making lots of money. Dairy producers wanted a new law to give them higher payments. Cotton farmers believed themselves better off with nothing new but were convinced that some legislation was bound to pass and tried to make as good a deal as possible.

In June 1973 the Senate approved what was primarily a five-year extension of the old law with the added new concept of target prices. The president indicated that it would be vetoed. Earl Butz told the House Agriculture Committee he could accept target prices as a method of freeing farmers from direct government assistance, if the targets were lower than market prices so for at least two years the program would cost the government nothing, and if they were below production costs so farmers wouldn't be encouraged to grow for the government.

Already the coalition that traditionally helped pass farm

legislation was breaking up, and even the farm interests were fighting among themselves. To get a bill through, people created tenuous alliances. When the Senate limited farm payments to $20,000, depriving large cotton farmers of loopholes that had allowed payments to go to relatives and friends, the cotton people frantically searched for allies. In the House they joined the administration's supporters to defeat an escalator clause linking target prices to annual production costs. This alliance did not give cotton all the votes it needed, however, so when the House considered a farm bill that also denied food stamps to strikers and their families, traditionally anti-union cotton people made an alliance with labor's supporters.

On July 19 the House passed its version. *Congressional Quarterly* said, "Stumbling around in an uncertainty that bordered on chaos, the House passed a farm bill . . . after voting several times in favor of amendments that seemed to deny the bill any chance of passage." The bill then went to conference. In that committee the representatives of both House and Senate, strongly influenced by threats of a presidential veto, resolved 110 out of the 111 differences between House and Senate bills. That left only the issue of food stamps for strikers. On July 31 the Senate approved the conference compromise without the food-stamp ban.

On August 3, after receiving assurances from Earl Butz that Nixon would sign the bill, Representative W. R. Poage (a Democrat from Texas and chair of the House Agriculture Committee) offered a motion to accept the Senate version. It was late in the day, and the House was about to adjourn for a month-long vacation. Even though the House had voted three times to retain the provision banning food stamps for strikers, Poage's motion passed, including a new amendment urging farmers to produce as much as possible. The amendment was meaningless, but because of parliamentary rules, no additional amendments could be introduced to reinstate the ban on food stamps. Poage explained that his new amendment was necessary to pass a new farm law.

Northern Democrats, pleased by the food-stamp retention and Southern Democrats, believing that this was better than nothing, voted strongly in favor of the bill. Republicans voted 2-to-1 against it, angry because of Poage's parliamentary tactics and because they thought the act would subsidize too many farmers. Representative Silvio O. Conte (a Republican from Massachusetts) said, "It is time for the Congress to enact a farm bill without allowing secret tradeoffs . . . and parliamentary ploys that block the will of the majority. It is time we stopped selling the consumer down the river to make a handful of fat cat corporate farmers even richer." On August 10, 1973, President Nixon signed the bill.

Later Earl Butz pointed to that law and to the concept of target prices, which was not his, as the centerpiece of his legislative victory in getting the government out of agriculture. No representative or senator who voted either for or against the Agriculture and Consumer Protection Act of 1973 challenged that claim.

That was the first time Congress passed a farm bill that did not deal with the problems of surplus. "For nearly forty years," Earl O. Heady wrote in his 1967 book, *A Primer on Food, Agriculture, and Public Policy*, "the United States has been plagued with food surpluses in one form or another. . . . Aside from shipment of surplus food as food aid, the policies in effect . . . , under both Republican and Democratic administrations, are variations of those initiated in 1933. . . . Even with these . . . persistent efforts, we have not come to a long-run solution of the nation's basic farm problems. Left to the market alone, with complete elimination of public programs and outlays, output would erupt, prices would be greatly depressed, and many farmers would go bankrupt in the short run."

Suddenly surplus—the cause of the nation's "basic farm

problems" — was gone. The farm policies that dealt with that problem were no longer being used. For the first time in nearly 50 years most farmers depended entirely on market prices for their income, and since prices were high, farmers welcomed their record prosperity and wanted more.

Less than two years later the same Congress attempted to reimpose the restrictions and the comprehensive system of government payments that the 1973 act had lifted. By then the situation had changed too much for the reimposition to be effective, and besides, it was vetoed.

Two months after the agriculture act passed, in October 1973, the Organization of Petroleum Exporting Countries imposed an embargo on oil exports that lasted until March 1974. The price of petroleum quadrupled, and supplies were hard to find. The nightly news showed long lines of cars whose drivers waited hours to get gas. Nixon created a new energy agency with sweeping powers to control oil prices and allocate supplies. Even though agriculture received priority treatment, the embargo's effect on the farm community was comprehensive and lasting; in America's capital-intensive system of farming, petroleum was the largest single raw ingredient. Not only did farmers have trouble finding gas to run their tractors, harvesters, and trucks, there was a shortage of petroleum-based fertilizers. From 1972 to 1974 fertilizer costs rose by up to 1000 percent, and farmers were forced to reduce the amount of fertilizer they used. Crops suffered. Production costs skyrocketed. Wheat farmers who could profitably sell for less than $1.50 a bushel only a year earlier suddenly needed at least $3.50 to break even.

Meanwhile the embargo devastated developing nations. India and Bangladesh often could not find or afford petroleum-based fertilizers, and they could not operate irrigation pumps. Throughout the world 1973 was a horrible year; bad weather got worse, agricultural productivity declined after two decades of steady growth, and already

poor crops were starved by the energy crisis. In some countries scarce foreign currency had covered only increased
petroleum costs for basic services. Threatened with food
shortages and mass starvation, these countries were
desperate for both grain and the cash to buy it.

The United States responded to the crisis in 1974 by lifting acreage restrictions on domestic sugar production,
canceling and restricting large export grain sales, cutting
back on food aid, and issuing a report that vividly described
what food shortages would be like if they occurred at home.

In June 1974 Congress gave Earl Butz his second major
legislative victory; the House narrowly failed to renew the
Sugar Act. Pressure from the newly powerful consumer
movement shattered the traditional farm alliance that north-
eastern and pro-union Democrats had previously had with
their more conservative rural colleagues. For the first time
since 1934, restrictions on domestic sugar acreage and on
imports were lifted, and the marketplace instead of the
Department of Agriculture determined the price of sugar.
Nevertheless sugar jumped from a wholesale price of 11
cents a pound to 60 cents a pound in less than a year.

Skyrocketing sugar prices proved the largest single factor in that year's 12.2 percent rise in food prices. Americans
ate more sugar than any other single commodity—more
than 120 pounds a year per citizen. Suddenly they stopped taking it for granted. In 1974 it was discussed by front-
page newspaper articles, network news programs, government agencies, and talk-show hosts. Even television commercials focused on the high prices and fear of shortages.

In October 1974, in the midst of major crop failures, the
administration considered the recent sale of 3.4 million tons
of grain to the Soviet Union and was afraid that there might
not be enough to feed the American people. President Ford
imposed an embargo—technically a "voluntary restraint"
by asking Earl Butz to ask Continental Grain and Cook
Industries to cancel their sales contracts. He also requested

that all grain traders receive prior approval from the Agriculture Department before making major sales.

Later Senator Henry Bellmon asked the president of a trading company whether he had stopped selling voluntarily. "It is kind of like your wife asking, 'Dear, would you mind handing me that glass?' And you voluntarily do it," Edward W. Cook, president of Cook Industries, said. "That is the kind of voluntary system that you had in that sort of deal. You might as well face it. When the President of the United States or the Secretary of Agriculture calls me up and says, 'Mr. Cook, would you please,' that is the same situation I run into at home every night when mixing my wife a drink. Some days I really do not want to do it, but I do."

Senator Bob Dole of Kansas, later an outspoken critic of agricultural embargoes, explained that this one was necessary. "The consumers of this country need assurances that a foreign country will not come into our market and buy up all our food."

Also in October the House Agriculture Committee issued "Malthus and America," a report that said there could be massive food shortages in the United States and abroad. "Did you ever stop to think," the report asked, "what the effects on our national security would be if, say, the governments of three or four major countries collapsed due to a shortage of food, resulting in riots in the streets and an overthrow of the government?" The report continued, "Will America allow a food shortage to surprise us . . . and only then react *after* we find people standing in line from 7 a.m. to 9 a.m. on Tuesday and Thursday mornings waiting to get into their local grocery store to buy a limited quantity of food?"

Not only did a major drought help cause the worst crop failures in the United States in nearly 40 years, but there were other disappointments as well. For years everyone assumed that the government was paying farmers not to grow on fertile land. Then the government stopped its payments, and in 1974, for the first time in decades, farmers tried to achieve full production — what insiders at the USDA called "wall-to-wall planting." Much of the new land turned out to be infertile. Of the 62 million acres the government had paid to take out of production, only 37 million were productive. Agriculture experts had believed that the unused acres were a reserve the world could rely on in times of famine, but in 1974 they found, as President Ford later put it, that the reserve was "illusory." At the same time the Department of Agriculture's estimates, relied on for major policy decisions, turned out to be consistently wrong and optimistic. By the end of 1974, the USDA was found to have overestimated the size of the corn crop by 1.5 billion bushels.

Despite fears of major domestic shortages the American people had enough food. In 1974 meat consumption set a new record at nearly 117 pounds per person. Meanwhile world leaders were afraid there would be massive starvation worldwide.

In November 1974 the United Nations sponsored the World Food Conference in Rome, which convened under a crisis atmosphere. Amid predictions that 10 million people would die of starvation in 1975 and hundreds of millions would die within 10 years, delegates discussed the current widespread famine in Bangladesh, India, and the sub-Sahara region of North Africa. U.N. Secretary General Kurt Waldheim asked, "How did the world drift into this grievous condition?" Thirty-two countries defined by the United Nations as "most seriously affected" by the famine urgently needed 7 million additional tons of grain to stave off immediate catastrophe. Eventually the United States helped supply the grain, but with an inadvertent touch of black comedy this country announced that it was immediately sending 5000 tons of fortified fallout-shelter survival biscuits (described as old but not stale) to Bangladesh.

The Rome conference highlighted the sudden change in the issue of world hunger. For decades starvation had occurred despite an abundance of food because of poverty, inadequate distribution, illiteracy, governmental inefficiency, and corrupt officials' diverting food assistance to enrich themselves. Then policy-makers examined rising population figures and declines in crop production and became afraid that the world was no longer capable of producing enough to feed itself. The conference frequently focused on the poor countries bankrupted by the high price of oil and unable to afford the increasingly expensive grain. The issue of money was eclipsed by the issue of supply, however. Suddenly grisly scenarios were being seriously discussed for apportioning limited food resources. How many millions should be allowed to die of starvation, and in what countries should the deaths occur?

In August 1974 the Central Intelligence Agency had predicted that the world's poorest countries would become "ever more dependent on U.S. food exports" and that "as custodian of the bulk of the world's exportable grain" the U.S. could "regain its primacy in world affairs." Secretary of State Henry Kissinger observed, "Until 1972, we thought we had inexhaustible food surpluses and the fact that we have to shape our policy to relate ourselves to the rest of the world did not really arise until 1973." Early in 1975 President Ford observed, "Much has been made during this past year about a possible Malthusian crisis in the less developed countries. Population is growing at quite high rates in these countries and has done so since World War II. Unless the growth of population slows, many question whether the necessary large increases in agricultural output can be achieved in the future. The upsurge in commodity prices these last 2 years and the famine conditions in the African Sahel and in South Asia bolster these fears. . . . "

In 1975 Willard W. Cochrane of the University of Minnesota told the Joint Economic Committee of Congress, "There is no question that the short crop in 1972 was what shot prices up. . . . But the grain market, the world grain market, had been tightening for several years and this was simply . . . the straw that broke the camel's back. In 1968 I wrote a book . . . in which I . . . felt that we could at least through the 1970s and 1980s produce all we needed. . . . I have changed my views since 1968."

In January 1975 *The New York Times Magazine* published a cover story entitled "Again 'Triage' — Who Shall Live? Who Shall Die?" Triage, from the French verb for "to sort," was a term originally used by medical units in World War I. When supplies were limited, the wounded were divided into three groups. The only people treated were those who needed immediate attention and were thought likely to recover. It was considered a waste of valuable supplies to care for people who would either recover without medical treatment or die even if they were treated.

Author Wade Greene suggested that with "severe food shortages in many parts of the world today" the following "bleak" and "unthinkable" scenario was likely: "The world is swept by famine as the populations of many regions outstrip their agricultural capacities. Only one nation, the United States, has a sizable surplus of food. And, with godlike finality, we dispense it, after systematically deciding which people are salvageable and should be fed, which will survive without help, and which are hopeless and should be left to the ravages of famine."

He cited the congressional testimony of Professor John Steinhart, from the University of Wisconsin, who said, "I guess I would argue that we are already practicing triage, whether we call it by that name or not. The decision, for instance, that the President not respond to Secretary Butz's or Senator Humphrey's request for additional food for India, but, instead, supply some additional food to Syria means a triage decision. That decides that some Indians will die and some Syrians will live. It is as simple as that."

Greene suggested that, since the U.S. was currently practicing triage in some form, it ought to be done consciously and intelligently with full public debate on the moral priorites involved.

Triage became a trendy concept, especially among liberals. Senator Edward Kennedy (a Democrat from Massachusetts) inserted it in speeches on college campuses. Meanwhile the concept of "food power," the same thing as triage only expressed differently, seemed especially attractive to conservatives. President Ford later called it "agripower." On December 15, 1975 *Business Week's* cover story was "U.S. Food Power, Ultimate Weapon in World Politics?" A high level State Department official said, "We have the food and the hell with the rest of the world."

By the end of 1975 the U.S. was harvesting bumper crops; by the following year world crops improved, and once again agricultural shortage was replaced by surplus. Triage and "food power" became yesterday's headlines. Harold O. Carter, Professor of Agricultural Economics at the University of California, observed, "Certainly the dire predictions that were made by many notables at the opening [of the World Food Conference] last November that millions of people would die of starvation before mid-1975 have proven to be exaggerated."

At the conference itself, however, the temptation to believe the pessimists had been overwhelming. There world attention had focused on the U.S. because despite crop losses, rising domestic prices, and embargoes, this country was the world's major food exporter. It controlled more than 50 percent of the grain in world trade, most of which went to the Third World. Three bushels of wheat went to developing countries for every one to industrialized countries.

Earl Butz emerged from the conference with his public image blackened but his power intact. The world was pressuring the U.S. to increase its food aid. Butz, who declared this country was not "the world's father provider," held fast to his hard-line position that food aid fosters dependency, and the key to overcoming shortages was to increase productivity. He argued that retreating from the administration's basic policy of requiring countries to pay for grain would further damage their own agricultural economies while at the same time depriving this one of badly needed revenue. Secretary of State Henry Kissinger told the conference, "No tragedy is more wounding than the look of despair in the eyes of a starving child," but he supported Butz's view, reluctant to diminish further the leverage food assistance gave to foreign policy.

One major point of leverage was the Food for Peace program, which had been created in 1954 as the Farm Surplus Disposal Act, Public Law 480. After the Korean War the U.S. needed some way to dispose of commodities whose surpluses were swollen by recent advances in herbicides, seed strains, and other technologies. Title II of the act provided donations to "needy" countries. The Department of Agriculture donated its surpluses or bought supplies for the occasion, which the U.S. distributed either directly or through CARE, the Catholic Relief Fund, and other voluntary organizations. Title I provided long-term loans to foreign governments, which then negotiated purchase prices and delivery costs directly with the multinational grain traders.

In the 1960s President Kennedy called PL 480 "Food for Peace," but despite the catchy name, the program's purpose was still primarily to dispose of surpluses. Little thought was given to its effect on developing countries.[2] By the 1970s critics from all political spectrums were pointing out that farmers in developing countries had been unable to compete with free and cheap food. As a result of Food for Peace, farmers were forced off the land, and countries with limited income became increasingly dependent on U.S. exports.

Having fostered dependency, Earl Butz, President Ford, and others decided that the best long-term solution was to make increased dependence unattractive, which in turn, they hoped, would eventually force self-sufficiency. In the early '60s Food for Peace disposed of 16 million tons a year. By 1975 the figure was 6 million tons. In 1974, at the height of the world crisis, the U.S. cut back on international aid so that there were 19 million fewer people receiving free food than in 1973. Until 1970 Food for Peace subsidized 50 percent of the U.S. exports to developing nations. By 1975 the figure was down to 15 percent, and the countries paid commercial prices for grain.

Meanwhile American farmers were being forced back into the marketplace. The secure PL 480 market had encouraged many farmers, especially rice producers, to neglect their marketing skills and "grow for the government." At the same time the State Department, which eventually administered the program although funds from the Department of Agriculture paid for it, used it as a tool in foreign policy. In 1974 fewer than half the countries that received free Food for Peace shipments were on the U.N.'s list of the 33 countries "most seriously affected" by hunger. Instead both free food and the loan program were used to influence policy. For example when a right-wing regime replaced the Allende government in Chile, Richard Nixon shipped large quantities of PL 480 aid. When Congress refused to authorize further arms for Vietnam and Cambodia, the administration provided commodities that were traded for arms.

Nor was the program immune to congressional abuses. Representative Otto Passman (a Democrat from Louisiana), chair of the Subcommittee on Foreign Operations, pressured foreign diplomats to buy rice instead of the wheat that, at the time, could feed twice as many for the same price. He traveled around the world with Tongsun Park, whom he identified as an agent for the rice trade, introducing Park to officials of foreign governments. *The Washington Post* reported that Passman "has been known to summon diplomats to his office, discuss their countries' food deficit problems and extol the virtues of American rice. 'The message is clear,' said one diplomat." Passman's subcommittee had jurisdiction over the Food for Peace program.

By the 1970s Food for Peace had become discredited. Prominent experts questioned whether it might not make more sense to scrap the program and reconsider the world's needs.

In February 1975, when the world was still worried about food shortages, Senator Milton Young (a conservative Republican from North Dakota) worried that by summer record crops would drive prices down. Farmers said that unless something were done immediately to reduce production and help prices, they would experience the worst farm crisis since the Depression. "The farmers in my State," Young said, "the wheat producers, are worried about surpluses now. In fact, the Farm Bureau [a conservative farm group] and the NFO [National Farmers Organization, a liberal farm group] are urging farmers to cut wheat acres from 15 to 30 percent."

Recognizing that voluntary efforts traditionally fail, as this one did, Congress passed a one-year "emergency" farm bill, the Agriculture and Anti-Depression Act of 1975.

On May 1 President Ford vetoed the bill despite fellow Republicans' advice to the contrary. Earl Butz had threatened to resign if Ford signed. Butz gambled that by the time harvest came, farmers would find a market for their grain. Farmers, looking at falling prices, were frightened because they depended entirely on the marketplace for their income, and they had borrowed heavily on the assumption that high prices would hold. A politically astute staff member for the House Agriculture Committee predicted, "Unless Butz does something to raise wheat and corn prices, he will be driven out of office." A spokesperson for the Department of Agriculture admitted, "Farmers sat on a razor blade this year. Frankly, there was some sweat on foreheads here in the early part of July." A grain cooperative ran a full-page newspaper advertisement in *The Washington*

Post headlined, "Cheap Food Could Starve Us to Death." It said, "Realistically, we can't expect farmers to continue producing food that doesn't produce adequate capital to buy the equipment and supplies for the next year's crops."

In July the Russians arrived, like the cavalry, to rescue the agricultural economy with even larger purchases than in 1972. Again they made the largest agricultural purchase in history — 14.6 million tons of American grain. The sale saved American farmers from surpluses, but again agricultural policy-makers worried about shortages. Much of the grain had not even been harvested, and severe summer drought and floods in the Midwest had had as-yet-unknown effects. Again the USDA's estimates of both America's and Russia's crop sizes proved unreliable and optimistic.

On August 11 President Ford, despite strenuous objections from Butz, ordered the sales to stop. The president was convinced there was a real danger the Russians might own America's healthy corn crop while the U.S. would have to buy it back to feed the American people.

Irate farmers interrupted President Ford's golfing vacation in Colorado to ask him to lift the embargo; they said they depended on exports for survival. In July the price of food rose at an annual rate of 22.4 percent for the second month in a row, and President George Meany of the AFL-CIO blamed Soviet purchases. In August longshore workers in Houston refused to load Soviet-bound wheat. Butz publicly blamed the featherbedding practices of unionized intermediaries for much of the rise in food costs, but he admitted that the Russian sale would cost American consumers an additional 1.5 percent. Farmers, dissatisfied with established farm groups, set up an ad-hoc lobbying effort to convince the American people the grain exports were important.

The harvest proved the embargo had been unnecessary. The wheat and corn crops were the largest in American history. But the Russian sales — despite consumer groups' opposition to them — demonstrated how much our agriculture depended on exports. By 1975 it was clear that the survival of American agriculture required exporting two-thirds of the wheat crop, one-quarter of the corn, and more than half the soybeans. Exported food was America's single largest source of foreign exchange, and the economy as a whole needed the income to pay for petroleum and other imported goods.

The embargo, originally supposed to protect this country from food shortages, was retained until October to modify the Soviets' behavior while building political support for exports. Throughout late summer and early fall 1975 the Department of Agriculture said the problem was not Soviet purchases, but erratic Soviet buying habits. The Japanese, our largest grain customers, were called model trading partners; from 1970 to 1976 they bought 70 million tons of grain from the U.S. while the Russians only bought 38 million tons. The difference between the two was that the Japanese were predictable and consistent, while the Russians came in and out of the market suddenly, buying little in some years and in others disrupting the process with their massive purchases.

On October 20, while President Ford was in bed with the flu, the White House announced that the embargo was lifted; the U.S. and the Soviet Union had reached a joint agreement on grain sales. Each year for the next five years, the Soviets agreed to purchase at least 6 million metric tons of wheat and corn. If they wanted to buy more than 8 million tons, they would need to go through a routine procedure for advance permission. In return they agreed to sell the U.S. 10 million tons of oil a year at a price to be negotiated. Each side tacitly understood that no oil would ever be sold, and none was. By apparently linking petroleum to grain, an idea newly in fashion (where it stayed for about a year), President Ford hoped to soften domestic opposition. The Soviets' agreement to buy regularly also helped. Meanwhile mounting agricultural surpluses allayed consumers' primary fear that exports threatened the food supply.

Farmers worried that the series of embargoes had hurt markets abroad. Foreign customers might be reluctant to buy from the U.S., which had shown itself to be an unreliable supplier. The Japanese, the Russians, and others might go first to other grain-producing countries such as Argentina, Canada, and Australia. Especially when it had large surpluses, the U.S. did not want to become a "residual supplier" to be used only after preferred sellers exhausted their inventories. This status would lower farm income for years and would require U.S. farmers to pay high storage costs. In 1980, when President Carter embargoed grain sales to protest the Soviet invasion of Afghanistan, that is precisely what happened.

On February 6, 1976, Congress gave Earl Butz his last legislative victory by lifting planting restrictions on rice. With some minor exceptions — peanuts, tobacco, and an obscure variety of cotton — the government no longer regulated the use of cropland.

On October 3, 1976, President Ford accepted Earl Butz's forced resignation after a racist, obscene remark became public knowledge. On the airplane coming back from the Republican convention Pat Boone had asked Earl Butz why the Republican party, the party of Abraham Lincoln, could not attract more black voters. (Boone is a singer most famous for his hits from the 1950s, such as "Love Letters in the Sand"; for wearing white "buck" shoes; and for preaching to teenagers on the virtues of sexual continence and wholesome family life.) Butz answered, "I'll tell you what coloreds want. It's three things: first, a tight pussy; second, loose shoes; and third, a warm place to shit. That's all!"

The remark was regarded as so obscene and offensive that *The New York Times* summarized it and only one daily newspaper printed it in full. In his resignation statement Earl Butz said the "joke" did not represent his true feeling.

Summarizing his accomplishments as secretary of agriculture, Earl Butz said, "Farmers have had the yoke of bureaucratic control lifted from them."

---

1. Richard Nixon resigned from office in August 1974. Gerald Ford then became president and kept Earl Butz as his secretary of agriculture. When Butz resigned in 1976 he had the most seniority in the cabinet. From the perspective of agricultural policy, Richard Nixon's resignation was merely a footnote.

2. Some people argued that the United States was thoughtfully and deliberately fostering dependence. However, because of the nature of the program, this conspiracy would have required more competence than government has. Also, it would have required compliance from such a patently nice person as Senator George McGovern, who once ran PL 480. It is difficult to believe that the man considered too liberal and not mean enough for the presidency deliberately caused children to starve so he could make a fast buck for grain farmers.

Chapter Seven

The Marketplace
Makes Policy

> "Our boss has thousands of people working for him and they all do something comprehensible. They take cocoa and sugar and milk and make it into chocolate. Amory Shaw is also a vice-president. He has one secretary, one assistant, and he spends his time buying and selling millions of dollars' worth of cocoa that doesn't exist."
>
> But Stratton was playing games with the wrong man. The New York City Police Department had handpicked their emissary.
>
> "You mean Shaw trades in futures on the Cocoa Exchange?" Udall asked politely.
>
> "I prefer to think of it as black magic."
>
> —*Sweet and Low*
> by Emma Lathen

When Earl Butz had finished lifting the "yoke of bureaucratic control" from farmers, the marketplace had replaced the government as the most important single determiner of our country's food policy. During the 1970s, however, there was a general lack of sophistication about such basic questions as: Where is the marketplace located? How is the price of a commodity, such as corn, determined? What is the difference between a "future" price and a "cash" price? What purpose does the market serve? At a White House press conference in

October 1975 a reporter asked Earl Butz, "Was there agree-ment of price on . . . grains going to Russia?" Butz said, "No, sir. The only agreement is that they move at market prices." The reporter clearly did not know what Butz was talking about and asked, "What market, Mr. Secretary?" Many observers reacted to Butz's incessant references to "the free market" as if it were some abstract concept like free love, so the "market" became, in the absence of a governmental agricultural policy, a euphemism for no policy at all.

In September 1975 Butz had appeared before the House Agriculture Committee with a copy of *The Wall Street Journal*. As part of a formal report on the "General Agricultural Situation," he opened up the newspaper and used it as a prop. Agricultural policy in the U.S., he boasted, was finally being determined by the marketplace. He said, "I . . . see that next May corn is selling for $3.24. . . . Do you think that they [farmers] will fail to read that signal?" He also read aloud the futures prices of wheat and soybeans.

The marketplace was as surprised by the change as everyone else.[1] Futures exchanges, such as the one in New York where sugar was traded, suddenly emerged from sleepy obscurity, having been used primarily as specialized finan-cial tools for the food industry and as places where speculators made offbeat investments. From 1955 to 1972, when sugar prices generally were less than 5 cents a pound, the New York Sugar Exchange experienced days when no sugar at all was bought or sold. Then a committee of five people decided what the price should be, making a kind of educated guess, and that became the price *The Wall Street Journal* reported.

In 1974, however, the Sugar Exchange came alive when prices jumped from 15 cents in January to 63 cents in November. Then a shrewd speculator, using the margin system common in futures trading, could have parlayed a $1200 investment into $65,632. For decades the sugar contract traded on the New York Sugar Exchange had not been based on the U.S.-grown stock because the government, not the marketplace, solely determined U.S. sugar policy. But with the demise of the Sugar Act in 1974, the exchange suddenly and unexpectedly was trading contracts for which millions of tons of U.S. sugar could be demanded.

Meanwhile the better-known exchanges such as the Chicago Board of Trade, which accounted for 52 percent of the total activity in the commodities market, were also experiencing boom times. In 1976 15 exchanges traded futures contracts worth $544 billion. From 1972 to 1976 the volume of futures contracts increased 136 percent. By 1976 there were more futures contracts traded than stocks, and a seat on the Chicago Board of Trade cost more than one on the New York Stock Exchange. In March 1976 *Business Week's* cover story, "Commodity Trading, More ... More ... More ... ," observed, "Investors who five years ago may not have known a pork belly from a pogo stick have discovered commodities because that is where the torrid action has been all through the 1970s — in soybeans in 1973, in sugar ... two years ago, in hogs and pork bellies last year, in wheat today. Price fluctuations in commodities can make a raging bull stock market look tame by comparison."

The commodities market is complicated but still understandable. Describing its operation is easiest by walking through a transaction, in this case following two speculators (whose only objective is to make a profit) named Dick and Jane.[2] Their hypothetical futures trade begins the day after Labor Day 1976, during the last month of Earl Butz's tenure as secretary.

Dick is a lobbyist in Washington, D.C. On September 7 he reads that Europe is suffering from the worst drought in recent history and decides to profit from the misfortune by speculating that the price of corn will go up. He reasons that European cattleraisers, faced with the loss of domestic corn and other feedgrains, will be forced to import more from the U.S., thus raising corn prices here.

Dick goes to the offices of Merrill Lynch Pierce Fenner & Smith, takes the elevator to the commodities department, and buys December corn by 2:15 P.M. Washington time, just before the closing bell rings at the Chicago Board of Trade. Dick buys the smallest quantity available—one contract, which is 5000 bushels. He pays $3.00-¼ (three dollars and one-quarter cent) per bushel. He will make or lose $12.50 for each quarter-cent change in price, the minimum fluctuation possible.

He has purchased future corn. Since he is buying December's corn in September, Dick cannot immediately obtain the corn. In theory if he waits until December, he can. In practice, since futures traders are in the market to profit on price fluctuations, Dick will cancel out his contract before delivery can take place.

At the same time Jane, a New York theatrical producer, goes to her broker, Conti Commodity Services. She thinks prices will fall by December because she believes a large U.S. crop will lower prices and the Europeans will slaughter off livestock rather than pay high feed costs. For weeks she has waited for corn to reach what she thinks will be seasonal highs before committing herself to speculating that the price will drop. On September 7 prices rise because of a report that dry weather in the corn belt may result in a smaller harvest than expected. Jane considers herself lucky that she was able, by closing bell, to sell Dick one contract at $3.00-¼ a bushel.

Jane lives in an apartment in New York City. She doesn't own either a farm or the corn she sold. In his biography of Frank Norris, Franklin Walker wrote, "Norris, who easily grasped the drama of the sales on the floor of the pit, . . . had difficulty comprehending how a man could sell a thousand bushels of wheat when he did not own them." Norris worked hard—he said it was the most difficult task he ever performed—to understand futures trading, because he was writing *The Pit,* the 1903 classic novel about abuses in trading. Nonetheless selling short—that is, selling a commodity one does not own—is easy.

On September 7, when Jane sells Dick corn, she makes a legally binding contract to deliver 5000 bushels to him in December. In theory where she gets the corn between September, when it may still be growing in Iowa, and December is her problem. She can buy it from a farmer, a warehouse operator or a grain merchant, as long as she can deliver the 5000 bushels in December. In practice Jane and other short sellers will not have a problem because—like Dick and the other buyers—they will almost certainly cancel out their contracts before delivery comes due.

When Dick's order is transmitted from Washington, a telephone rings on the fourth floor of the Chicago Board of Trade. The information that Dick wants to buy corn is handed to a runner, who dashes to the nearby corn "pit" to find the exchange member handling the Merrill Lynch account. In the pit people are trading in September 1976 futures, to be delivered in the middle of the month, and in contracts for delivery in December 1976 and in March, May, July, and September 1977. The members of the Chicago Board of Trade—called "floor brokers"—position themselves according to delivery date in the eight-sided wooden pit, which looks like a Hollywood version of a cockfighting ring. The runner finds the Merrill Lynch broker in the July 1977 side of the pit. The broker looks at Dick's order form and moves over to the December 1976 side.

Simultaneously Jane's order to sell is transmitted from New York to the Conti phone in Chicago, where a runner finds the floor trader, who moves from the March 1977 side to the December 1976 side. "All orders to buy or sell are made by public outcry," the Chicago Board of Trade explains, "so that any trader in the pit who wishes to take the opposite side of the trade may do so." That is, the traders call out the orders to buy and sell. As the closing bell is about to ring, the screaming becomes louder and the hand waving more frenetic. The Conti broker waves an arm in the air, hand clenched except for a single finger, indicating one contract for sale. "Ninety-nine," one trader screams, offering ninety-nine cents per bushel. Like a chorus the bidding continues, "Ninety-nine and a quarter." "Ninety-nine and three quarters." "Three dollars!" The Merrill Lynch trader points a single finger toward himself and yells even louder, "Three and a quarter." "Sold!" The bell rings, ending the trading day. Within minutes Dick and Jane receive teletyped confirmation that the trade was completed, and the next morning's paper reports $3.00-¼ as the closing price of corn at the Chicago Board of Trade.

When the market opens on September 8, there are predictions of rain for the Midwest, which may help crops that will be harvested within a month. If it helps, there will be more corn, and according to conventional wisdom the more there is, the lower the price will be. Reacting to the weather forecast, the market falls to a low of $2.93-½.

An emergency comes up with Jane's current Broadway production, and she decides to get out of the market. She buys 5000 bushels and is lucky to get it at the day's low.

She is no longer obliged to deliver corn to anyone. On Tuesday she sold corn she didn't have to Dick at $3.00-¼ bushel. On Wednesday she bought corn from someone else at $2.93-½. Since she bought as much as she sold, 5000 bushels, the transactions cancel each other out. Since she sold for 6-¾ cents per bushel more than she paid one day later, she made $337.50. Jane gambled that the price would go down and won.

Meanwhile Dick still has a legal contract obliging him to receive 5000 bushels of corn in December. Even though Jane is out of the market, the Chicago Board of Trade points out that "there is a party to every trade." As long as Dick is still holding on to the paper proving he bought 5000 bushels, someone else has another paper promising to deliver them. The drop in price on September 8 leaves Dick with two clear choices. He can get out of the market immediately, losing $337.50 but avoiding further losses; or he can wait, hoping the price will go up. He decides to stay.

On November 3 the market reacts to the presidential election with seasonal lows. The commodity page of *The New York Times* explains, "From Jimmy Carter's position statements on agriculture, many traders believe he intends to increase price supports and encourage the building up once more of large Government stocks." December corn is now selling for $2.49-¾ a bushel. Dick decides to get out. He bet the price would go up, but it went down 51 cents. He loses $2550 plus the broker's commission, but at least he's canceled out his position by selling as much as he bought and is now out of the market and out of the danger of losing more.

Dick lost $2550 by speculating in the smallest quantity available, one contract of 5000 bushels. It is common for speculators to trade a hundred contracts, so each quarter-cent change in price represents a loss or gain of $1250.

When Earl Butz read aloud the futures price of corn, he was describing the change in agricultural policy. The futures price was the commonly used yardstick for evaluating what the price of the farmer's corn would bring when it was ready for sale on the cash market. The cash market was where traders bought and sold physical corn, as opposed to the futures market where traders speculated on its price fluctuations. The futures market provided an approximation of actual worth because in theory (although rarely in practice) a buyer of futures corn could take delivery.

Suddenly the futures price, not the government, determined how much a farmer planted or whether anything was planted at all. When the government had determined agricultural policy, a farmer could plant corn knowing that no matter what price he received at harvest time, the government's payments would ensure enough income to repay bank loans and other production costs. With the government out of agriculture, a farmer's survival suddenly depended entirely on price, not only on the cash price of corn that would be harvested in September, but also (since loans might be necessary for supplies) on the futures price to gauge the worth of corn to be planted the following May and harvested the following September. The farmer (or the banker) who saw that the price was too low might want to grow soybeans, cotton, or some other crop instead.

It was not enough to have a rough estimate of prices in five months or a year, however. When one's survival depended on a given price, an unexpected change could bring disaster. A commodity column in *The Wall Street Journal* in October 1975 described how daily changes in price on cash markets made it difficult for wheat farmers to decide when to sell their crop: "After usually selling part of the crop to pay production bills, 'each one of them watches the market like a hawk with his own target in mind,' says Roderick Turnbull, a Kansas City Board of Trade official. . . . Grain buyers add that the target is often as hard to hit as a Kansas quail. 'Steady $4 wheat would probably fill up my elevator,' says a Kansas broker, 'but if prices blow by that in a hurry, like maybe to $4.25, a farmer's going to sit on the whole pile for an even higher price until he figured out what happened. On the other hand, we've been down to $3.75 so often, he'd just sit there until it bounced back again. But dropping to $3.50 might shake him up. You tell me what it's worth.' "

As a result of this kind of uncertainty, farmers became increasingly sophisticated about offsetting risk. A common technique was to sign a contract, called a "forward contract," to deliver some or all of the unharvested crop. Even before planting, a farmer could contract to deliver a quarter of the corn harvest at $4 a bushel to a corn-flake manufacturer or a feed company the following September. Forward contracts reportedly became popular with Japanese businesspeople when the 1973 embargo to Japan made them worry about the reliability of supplies. The contract gave a farmer a guaranteed income and the buyer a guaranteed supply, and the futures market made it easy to arrive at a mutually agreeable price.

A more traditional method of offsetting risk was to hedge on the futures market (from the expression "to hedge one's bet"). A farmer whose decision to plant was based on receiving $3 a bushel—the price in *The Wall Street Journal*—ensured against a drop in price by selling short on corn contracts at $3 per bushel on the Chicago Board of Trade. If the price dropped to $2.20 the following September, the farmer could buy future corn, canceling out the contracts and receiving an 80-cent-a-bushel profit. Without that profit the drop to $2.20 on the corn to be harvested next September would be disastrous. With hedging, the money lost on the crop would be balanced out by profits on the futures market. On the other hand, if prices went up, then the losses on the futures market would be balanced out by profits on the crop. By hedging, the farmer had, in effect, obtained insurance protecting the $3 price of corn.

Similarly, industrial consumers needed to protect themselves from price increases. If a feed company signed a contract with a chicken producer to deliver feed made from corn in 12 months based on a price of $3 a bushel, the company needed to protect itself from having to pay more to obtain that corn. So at the same time that it contracted to sell feed, it bought future corn, thus ensuring that its profits or losses on the futures market would balance out when it bought cash corn.[3]

So futures markets can protect farmers against sudden declines in price, protect manufacturers against sudden increases, and reward people willing to assume the risks of speculating in price fluctuations.

Because of unprecedented interest in agriculture, congressional hearings and studies made it possible for the first (and thus far the only) time to form a comprehensive view of how corn moved from the farm to domestic and foreign buyers during the 1970s. In 1976 corn was the largest crop in the country. This was not the "vegetable corn" used for corn-on-the-cob or for canning. Rather, this corn was used to feed animals, either by the farmer directly or more commonly by animal farmers who bought the corn when corn farmers sold it in the marketplace. About 84 percent of sales were made to the corn farmers' local grain elevators, which are simply warehouses with facilities for loading and unloading. They are called elevators because when the corn is dumped from the farmer's truck into an unloading pit, a vertical conveyor belt with scoops elevates the grain to the top of the tall building. From the top the corn falls down a spout into a long, narrow, missile-shaped compartment for storage. To unload into a truck, railroad car, or barge the conveyor belt takes the grain from the bottom of the compartment up to the top and out the spout. (If farmers were dissatisfied with the local price, they could decide to pay to ship their crops to cash markets at Kansas City, Minneapolis, Chicago, or elsewhere.)

From America's 8000 country elevators, corn and other grains generally moved to 450 large elevators, called inland terminals, near major transportation centers to be stored until they were shipped to domestic and foreign customers.

In 1976 25 percent of the corn crop was exported, moving directly from country elevators or from inland terminals to the nation's 80 large, sophisticated port elevators and loaded into ocean-going vessels. Sixty percent of this country's grain exports left from ports on the Gulf of Mexico.

At New Orleans, the largest grain port in the world, five of the six principal trading companies owned elevators. The Cook elevator held 4.5 million bushels of grain, the Bunge elevator 8.6 million, together holding more than the entire year's production of a corn-producing county in Iowa. At the rate of 70,000 bushels an hour the Cook elevator often unloaded into huge supertankers — originally built to carry petroleum — whose storage capacity the company president compared to Washington's 15-story Madison Hotel. At the foreign port a vacuum sucked the grain out of the ship.

Not all the corn was the same, however. The marketplace depends on a grading system. In a bushel of Number 2 yellow corn, most kernels are whole and unbroken, the moisture level is low, and there is little dirt. When farmers sell their crop they have it husked and dried, a relatively simple process, and the selling price is based on the quality of their corn compared to Number 2 yellow. The futures contracts traded at the Chicago Board of Trade assume that if a corn buyer insisted on delivery, he or she would receive Number 2 yellow. This grading is necessary so traders can buy and sell commodities of equal value and so pricing decisions are based on corn that is uniform and interchangeable. All Number 2 yellow corn is identical, and it does not matter to the purchaser where it comes from. ("Fungible" is the market term that describes the uniformity and interchangeability without which futures and cash markets could not operate.)

Grading standards protect the honesty of the futures price. Even though more than 99 percent of all futures contracts cancel out, the contracts still have to resemble what people are actually willing to pay for the commodity. On delivery day, when traders frantically cancel out their positions so no one has to deliver or take delivery, the price of future corn and cash corn are the same. Otherwise, if the price of cash corn were higher, the buyers would insist on taking delivery and could then resell the corn for profit. If the price of cash corn were lower, the sellers could buy that and, at a profit, deliver the corn. Everyone knows delivery is based on the Number 2 yellow standard.

Frequently futures exchanges also house cash markets.

In 1976 the cash markets at the Chicago Board of Trade were across the room from the futures pits for corn, wheat, soybeans, and oats. The cash market consisted of a little-noticed row of high black tables, similar to worktables in old chemistry laboratories, where members wearing lab-like coats sat on stools. Messengers brought sandwich-sized bags with grain samples for the members to examine. The samples came from bonded warehouses where corn and other grains were stored and, if necessary, graded. The members worked for clients such as International Corn Products Company, which uses corn to make Argo Corn Starch and Karo Syrup. After evaluating a sample, the member decided how much to pay.

As long as the market based on prices established in the futures pits was honestly run, it reflected what food was worth. The futures pits permitted a broad range of interests, including farmers, industrial consumers, multinational grain-trading companies, foreign buyers, and speculators, to participate in establishing price. Price became the primary instrument of agricultural policy.

In theory agricultural policy is supposed to satisfy the country's and the world's food needs. It is supposed to provide adequate supplies so everyone will have enough to eat. It is supposed to protect against both oversupply and shortages so farmers' incomes are not hurt by low prices, and consumers are not hurt by high prices. The balance between high and low prices guarantees that farmers can continue to produce and consumers can continue to eat.

Before Earl Butz's tenure the government was not doing an effective job of implementing agricultural policy. Consumers didn't especially notice governmental inefficiency, except in the high taxes they paid to support farm programs, because they were the primary short-term beneficiaries. Because grain prices were extremely low, for example, farmers used grain to increase production of livestock for meat. This made retail prices low for animal products, encouraging Americans to increase per capita meat consumption and to rely on commercial products that used a lot of meat, such as fast foods, restaurant meals, and convenience foods.

In 1972 grain prices being low during a world shortage emphasized how ineffective governmental agricultural policy was, especially considering that millions of acres were being withheld from production. At some point the combined world food shortages and increased price of petroleum would have forced the government to change its policies, in turn forcing consumers to pay a higher price for food, perhaps encouraging them to modify their diets. (The pressure would have had to be strong, however. Even though retail food prices increased more than 50 percent from 1972 to 1976, in 1976 the U.S. per capita expenditure on food, as a percentage of income after taxes, was still the lowest in the world.) But policy-makers' slow response pointed out the need for an agricultural system that reflected changing conditions more rapidly.

Whatever the deficiencies of the marketplace, it established the only framework the country had for providing adequate supplies at moderate prices. Congress had effectively dismantled the programs that had made control possible, and although it remained continually willing to tinker with bailout programs for farmers, no one in Congress of either political party seriously proposed reestablishing comprehensive control over food policy. Congressional conservatives and liberals all agreed this control was impractical given demonstrated governmental inefficiency and the absence of significant political support.

No one denied that the market determined policy faster and more sweepingly than any regulator could. From 1971 to 1973, when average market prices jumped from $1.57 a bushel to $4.51 for wheat and from $1.27 to $2.92 for corn, farmers rapidly changed their practices. They grew as much grain as possible and increased their specialization, slaughtering livestock herds to concentrate on grain production. Livestock producers became more efficient, and many returned to feeding their herds on grass, which cheap grain had made unnecessary. Increased grain acreage made it possible to feed a world plagued by food shortages while earning the foreign-trade revenue to pay rising petroleum bills.

Ironically one of the clearest arguments in favor of letting the marketplace determine policy was made by Frank Norris, the most famous critic of its abuses. In his unfinished turn-of-the-century trilogy *The Epic of the Wheat*, Norris planned to show how food, the most elemental of powers, affects those who come into contact with it. In the first novel, *The Octopus,* Norris described the production of wheat on ten-thousand-acre plots of land. The office of one farmer is called "the nerve-center of the entire ten thousand acres. . . . and the most significant object in the office was the ticker. . . . During a flurry in the Chicago wheat pits in the August of that year. . . . Harran and Magnus had sat up nearly half of one night watching the strip of white tape jerking unsteadily from the reel." The mystical question asked in *The Octopus* — "When does wheat become wheat?" — is answered in *The Pit:* when the price is high enough. Norris intended to follow *The Pit* with a fictional account of how the wheat produced in California and "created" in Chicago is used, in Norris' words, for "relieving of a famine in an Old World Community"; but he died before writing it.

According to Norris the laws of supply and demand are natural forces; the futures markets translate the forces into price, and price "creates" food. The honest and successful speculator is in touch with the forces of nature and can anticipate how much food the world will need. Norris' character Curtis Jadwin became a hero because, contrary to the corrupt people around him, he believed prices should go up. By fighting against the manipulators and for the wheat, he encouraged farmers to plant more so people would have enough to eat. Because the power of nature was on his side, he was successful. When he became so obsessed by power that he fought against nature, however, he failed to control the market. His friend and broker told him, "I see that the farmers all over the country are planting wheat as they've never planted it before. Great Scott, J., you're fighting against the earth itself."

When Earl Butz read *The Wall Street Journal* to Congress, American agricultural policy had returned to the system Norris described in which the commodity ticker in the farmer's office determined how much he planted. This was the system the government replaced in 1933 because the abuses had been so spectacular. Forty years later, with the return to the marketplace, the bad reputation of the futures markets continued to influence the debate about our country's food policy.

In describing the turn-of-the-century period when the bad reputation began, the Chicago Board of Trade noted that it was "filled with incidents of public outrage against alleged speculative abuses in commodities." The most dramatic speculative abuse was cornering the market. *The Pit* was based on an actual 1897 attempt to corner the wheat market. Norris described his hero's success: "Then at last the news of the great corner, authoritative, definite, went out over all the country, and promptly the figure and name of Curtis Jadwin loomed suddenly huge and formidable in the eye of the public. There was no wheat on the Chicago market. He, the great man, the 'Napoleon of La Salle Street,' had it all. He sold it or hoarded it, as suited his pleasure. He dictated the price to those men who must buy it of him to fill their contracts. . . . By now the foreign demand was a thing almost insensate. There was no question as to the price. It was, 'Give us the wheat, at whatever cost, at whatever figure, at whatever expense; only that it be rushed to our markets with all the swiftness of steam and steel.' At home, upon the Chicago Board of Trade, Jadwin was as completely master of the market as of his own right hand. Everything stopped when he raised a finger; everything leaped to life with the fury of obsession when he nodded his head."

J. Blake Imel, an economist with the Commodity Futures Trading Commission, explained, "When you have a corner, you get absolute control of the deliverable supply." Theoretically it is possible to corner a market. Everyone who buys corn has a legal right to insist on delivery, but if everyone did that, there would not be enough corn to deliver. More than 99 percent of contracts cancel out, however, so delivery rarely occurs and is even more rarely a problem. Nonetheless Dick and Jane can illustrate how a corner works, assuming that Dick is very rich and gets away with breaking the law.

On the same September day Dick buys December corn from Jane, he also buys all the December corn anyone else is willing to sell. Simultaneously he buys warehouses full of cash corn. Between September and December he buys all the corn there is, which for his purposes is all the corn that can conceivably be delivered to Chicago (where everyone's contracts oblige them to deliver it) by December. Meanwhile Jane and others can't cancel out their futures positions, because they've sold corn to Dick, who by now holds most of the long contracts, and he won't let them buy back the corn they've sold. Come December he is holding on to all the contracts requiring delivery, and he says "Deliver!" But Jane and the other shorts can't deliver, because to do so they have to obtain corn from someone — a farmer, warehouse operator, or grain merchant. They can't because Dick owns all the corn there is. He has "absolute control of the deliverable supply." To satisfy their contractual obligation to deliver corn, the only solution for Jane and the other shorts is to agree to Dick's terms. He can charge whatever he wants. He has them in a corner.

Norris described the moment in April when his hero discovered the possibility of cornering the May wheat market:

> "'Why, look here,' he cried. 'Don't you see? Don't you see ____ ?'
>
> "'See what?' demanded the broker, puzzled by the other's vehemence. . . .
>
> "'Great Scott! I'll choke in a minute. See what? Why, I own ten million bushels of this wheat already, and Europe will take eighty million out of the country. Why, there ain't going to be any wheat left in Chicago by May! If I get in now and buy a long line of cash wheat, where are all these fellows who've sold short going to get it to deliver to me? Say, where are they going to get it? Come on now, tell me, where are they going to get it?'"

The fictional Curtis Jadwin succeeded in his corner, but the real character, on whose life the novel was based, failed. In 1897 Joseph Leiter bought all the nation's known supply of wheat. He raised the price so high the Russians ate rye and shipped their wheat to Chicago. Throughout the United States and the world, wheat that was not thought to exist appeared suddenly, as if by magic. Using tugs with steel prows, Armour plowed up the ice in the Great Lakes and moved 6 million bushels of wheat into Chicago in the middle of winter. Though Leiter finally owned 50 million bushels of wheat, he did not have "absolute control of the deliverable supply." When he could no longer afford to buy more, the wheat flooding Chicago lowered the price; his corner was destroyed, and he was ruined financially.

Although Leiter failed in his corner, he succeeded in "squeezing" the market, a term used to describe what is today illegal: manipulating the market for the purpose of artificially raising prices. Although "speculative abuses" in Chicago resulted historically in occasional successes for the longs, the most successful and consistently hated traders were the shorts, who bet that the price would go down and made sure it did. In 1881 farmers raised 406 million bushels of wheat and sold it for $1.20 a bushel. Bankers, responding to urban interests, encouraged farmers to acquire expensive machinery and expand production. By 1884 half the farms in Kansas and North Dakota and one-third of the farms in South Dakota, Minnesota, and Nebraska had mortgages. Wheat prices were down to 77 cents, and by 1889 they were down still lower to 69 cents while production had expanded to 504 million bushels. In ten years farmers received 30 percent less for growing 25 percent more.

Populists argued that the farmer was the victim of big-city interests whose greed hurt everyone but themselves. The argument is most succinctly stated in Norris' 1903 short story "A Deal in Wheat," in which the shorts artificially lowered prices so much that farmers had to sell their crops at a loss and eventually were forced off the land. Then the speculators took possession of the wheat and by manipulating supply, transferring it from one place to another and exporting it, they raised prices artificially high. As a result urban workers paid a fortune for bread even though the wheat was grown at little cost. During the climax of Norris' story his farmer hero, forced to sell his wheat for 62 cents a bushel and go into bankruptcy, stood all night long on a bread line. In the morning the bakery put up a sign explaining that because wheat (the same wheat the farmer raised) was selling for $2 a bushel, "there will be no distribution of bread from this bakery until further notice."

Norris said, "The farmer — he who raised the wheat — was ruined upon the one hand; the working-man — he who consumed it — was ruined upon the other. But between the two, the great operators, who never saw the wheat they traded in, bought and sold the world's food, gambled in the nourishment of entire nations, practised their tricks, their chicanery and oblique shifty 'deals,' were reconciled in their differences, and went on through their appointed way, jovial, contented, enthroned, and unassailable."

Although the populist argument was often accurate, it was also based on rural prejudices. Concepts and people alien to farm communities were automatically regarded as suspect. Because the speculative abuses were so great, people associated or seen to be associated with the abuses were also tainted. The populists, therefore, attacked exporters because they were depleting our food supply, bankers, and anyone involved with sophisticated financial arrangements. For the populists the instant stereotype for the big-city, internationally-connected banker fascinated by high finance was the Jew, and the populist anti-Semitism of the 1890s was often openly expressed. By the 1970s, when populist rhetoric was again invoked to attack the market system and people involved with it, the anti-Semitism continued but was more subtle. Whisperers, for example, pointed out that the president of Continental Grain was Jewish.

Before the century turned, agrarian interests in Iowa, Massachusetts, and other states successfully pressured legislatures to outlaw futures trading by redefining it as gambling. Courts overturned the laws, ruling that the trading was not wagering because the futures contracts were binding, and buyers could legally require delivery. In 1892 one futures trader bluntly told the *Chicago Tribune,* "It's legal and faro isn't." The direct populist attack reached its high point in 1893 when both houses of Congress passed a bill abolishing futures trading. Because of a technicality the bill was not sent to the president for signature. Even though the futures trading industry survived, its opposition continued.

In 1930, when President Hoover failed to persuade farmers to control supply voluntarily, he attacked the Chicago Board of Trade. "Politicians shrieked in protest,"

Cedric B. Cowing wrote in *Populist, Plungers, and Progressives,* "when the Soviet Government was discovered selling short in the Chicago Board of Trade. . . . The Soviet short selling furnished an opportunity to blame foreigners for the economic situation. It jibed well with the dubious thesis of President Hoover: that the Depression originated abroad, that the United States was the victim of international vicissitude." By 1931 a desperate President Hoover issued a plea against selling short. "It has come to my attention that certain persons are selling short in the commodity market, particularly wheat. . . . I am not expressing my view upon the economics of short selling in normal times, but in these times this activity has a public interest. . . . The intention is to take a profit from the loss of other people . . . even though the effect may be directly depriving many farmers of their rightful income."

When Franklin Roosevelt became president in 1933 the Depression, combined with speculative abuses, had destroyed the effectiveness and credibility of the futures markets. Government programs were needed to prevent chaos not only for farmers, but for the entire food industry.

Given this background one can appreciate the dramatic impact of a secretary of agriculture reading aloud from *The Wall Street Journal,* telling Congress that after 40 years of governmental control, the marketplace now told farmers what to do. *The Wall Street Journal* itself was still a symbol to 1970s populists of big-city interests that opposed farmers.

Even more surprising than Butz's dramatic reading, however, was the House Agriculture Committee's lack of reaction. The representatives did not seem surprised that the futures market suddenly controlled our country's agriculture, nor did they question its wisdom. Less than five years earlier such a reading would have provoked fervent denunciations and detailed listings of the marketplace's abuses from Agriculture Committee Chair W. R. Poage and other specialists on the committee. But Poage was no longer chair and the committee itself was rapidly losing its expertise on agricultural issues.

In fact, throughout the 1970s, Congress—despite an unusually high number of studies and hearings—made no clear and consistent attempt to understand how our country's food policy had changed, let alone conduct a debate or even a discussion of what was in the public's interest. Suddenly farmers, food producers, grain traders, and consumers were forced to depend on a system that had been relatively unused for some 40 years, and there was no comprehensive inquiry into the system's effectiveness. Farmers and their Washington-based organizations made no attempt to develop a clear position on the marketplace. Consumer groups did not understand it. The industrial consumers, especially the multinational corporations, hid from public view. Even Butz was content to assert that the "free market" was efficient without clearly explaining why. Neither supporters nor critics bothered to explain their position. Although everyone admitted the country's food policy had changed dramatically, not only was there no comprehensive debate, but the quality of information was poor, and there was little attempt to develop the information needed for informed decisions.

To discuss the issues involved, it was necessary to organize Congress' piecemeal reaction to problems it could not entirely ignore. The closest thing to debate on the direction of the country's food policy occurred in June 1976 when the Senate Subcommittee on Multinational Corporations, chaired by Frank Church (a Democrat from Idaho), held hearings on the role of the grain-trading companies.

That year the six major multinational traders handled about 90 percent of America's grain exports, accounting for a major portion of the country's crops. Two-thirds of the United States' wheat, one-quarter of its corn, and more than half its soybeans were exported. Agricultural exports increased from $9.4 billion in 1972 to $23.7 billion by 1977.

But no one knew what effect the six multinationals had in determining prices.

For example tens of thousands of companies and individuals were using the cash and futures markets to purchase and to hedge, but they did provide the American people with foodstuffs made from corn. But six companies bought almost 25 percent of the total corn crop. They simply acted as intermediaries for foreign buyers, and the buyers themselves frequently hedged or speculated on the future markets, probably including the Russians. Nevertheless the role of the multinationals in the marketplace raised questions.

Each company claimed that it used the market to obtain the best possible price and that competition among the six prevented anyone from dominating the market. "It's a dog-eat-dog competitive business if ever there was one," Vice President Walter Saunders of Cargill told the Church subcommittee. Other people wondered whether the six companies so dominated the marketplace that they had the greatest single impact on price, often controlling it and thereby determining our country's agricultural policy. Senator Dick Clark (a Democrat from Iowa) raised this concern at the subcommittee hearings. He said, "Many of the grain companies insist that their success and profitability are due to the stiff competitive climate existing in the trade. Nonetheless, information received thus far . . . suggests that cooperation and mutual understanding may have supplanted competition in some areas of business."

Having raised the question of the multinationals' impact on price, the subcommittee never learned the answer. But for the first time Congress found out how a grain-trading company operated.

The companies first came to public attention as a result of the 1972 Russian grain deal; they operated with great secrecy. Because five of the six were privately owned, they did not have to file basic information, such as who owned them and in what country, with the Securities and Exchange Commission or other governmental agencies. Four of the six operated in the U.S. as subsidiaries of foreign companies.

None of the six made much attempt to present its views on agricultural policy issues or to define its role, preferring to remain inaccessible to the press and to Congress. When a reporter asked Assistant Vice President George Hughes from Bunge—a company controlling about 12 percent of the grain trade in America and 20 percent in the world—whether it was correct as published that Bunge is a division of Bunge & Born, a Buenos Aires conglomerate, Hughes said, "No comment." The reporter asked, if Bunge was an affiliate of an Argentinean corporation, why was it listed in Dun and Bradstreet's *Million Dollar Directory* as a subsidiary of a Curaçao firm? Hughes said, "Figure it out for yourself." After about 20 minutes of such answers, Hughes reluctantly provided his name and said he was vice president in charge of advertising and public relations. Asked how much public relations he did, Hughes said, "Very little, as you can see."

Eventually this passion for secrecy was carried to arrogant extremes, forcing Congress to make at least a token effort to find out something about some of the major participants in our country's food policy. Senator Church explained, "No one knows how they operate, what their profits are, what they pay in taxes and what effect they have on our foreign policy—or much of anything else about them." Because Church's subcommittee had the power of subpoena, Cargill could not ignore the invitation to testify and describe its operation.

In 1976 Cargill, with corporate headquarters in Minneapolis, was the largest grain-trading company in the world. In 1974 it exported 29 percent of the U.S. wheat crop, 16 percent of the corn, 18 percent of the soybeans, 22 percent of the sorghum, 42 percent of the barley, and 32 percent of the oats. Although its primary business was trading grain, Cargill owned everything from chicken farms to soybean-processing plants. It leased land from farmers, owned grain elevators, and owned or leased railroad cars and river barges that take the goods to market. The company owned or leased ships and controlled port facilities throughout the world.

Vice President Saunders testified, "The owners of Cargill established a new corporate entity, Tradax International, in Panama. Organizing the new company in Panama enables us to conduct our trading activities in the international grain market on the same tax footing available to our major competitors." But Corporate Vice President William R. Pearce, once a special trade representative for President Nixon, pointed out that "Panama is not an ideal location for managing a trade business, and therefore that suggested the wisdom of negotiating a management arrangement with a firm that could be positioned in a market or in a country like Switzerland." Geneva was picked because, as Saunders explained, "It was centrally located, had excellent travel and communications facilities . . . possessed a multi-lingual tradition to match the international character of the grain markets, had a history of economic and political stability and of freedom from exchange controls and levied only limited corporate taxes."

In simpler terms the Minneapolis-based firm set up a dummy corporation in Panama to evade the payment of taxes. Then it set up a Swiss company called Tradax Geneva. The Panamanian company contracted with Tradax Geneva to coordinate Cargill's international organizations — Tradax England, Deutsche Tradax, and other companies in the 36 or so countries in which it did business.

It's all Cargill, but the complications have a major advantage. Unless you're inside, it's hard to know what's going on. After 1972 the Soviets buying American grain no longer went to Cargill in the U.S. Instead they bought from Tradax Geneva, which, as the Cargill people explained, was closer to the Soviet Union and could provide better service to the customer. This arrangement made it difficult to keep track of Soviet purchases; by law Cargill had to report its sale of American grain to Tradax Geneva, but there was no requirement that Tradax Geneva in turn report its Soviet purchases. The grain might come from elsewhere. It could come from Argentina, for example, with Tradax Argentina selling to Tradax Geneva selling to the Soviets.

The executives said that each of the Cargill subsidiaries had its own profit center, competing with its siblings. In fact, Cargill Chairman Erwin Kelm testified, Cargill sold as much as 50 percent of its grain to its own subsidiaries abroad. Vice President Saunders explained, "We operate as two separate companies. Tradax actually buys from Cargill, and, of course, Cargill sells to Tradax, so on any given day if Cargill happens to have the most competitive offer on the market, Tradax will buy from Cargill, and if they don't they'll buy from somebody else."

As a result there was no way for the United States, which imposed four embargoes from 1973 to 1976, to make an embargo effective. The government didn't know who was buying the grain or where it would finally go, and there was no way of even proving that it was American. Canadian, Argentinean, and American grain of the same grade is indistinguishable.

Given its structure, Cargill was neither American nor foreign. It was owned by the 33 members of the Cargill and MacMillan families, some of the richest families in the U.S., who are descended from Will Cargill; he founded the company when he opened up a country elevator in Conover, Iowa, in 1865. The descendants did not own Cargill directly, but instead owned 70 percent of Tradax International in Panama, a holding company that owned 100 percent of the subsidiary companies. Cargill in Minneapolis was only the

American subsidiary of Tradax International. The remaining 30 percent of the holding company was owned by the Salevia Foundation in Switzerland, established by the members of the Cargill and MacMillan families. The 33 family members were also beneficiaries of the Swiss trust.

This information was only some of the attraction at Senator Church's hearings. Farmers and farmers' representatives from North Dakota provided an atmosphere of debate. North Dakota produced 15 percent of the nation's wheat. "Farmers like the so-called free market system," Myron Just, North Dakota's agriculture commissioner, testified, "but they think they are the only ones operating freely and openly in the market." The farmers believed they were being cheated by big-city interests. "The pyramid of power, as I see it," Just said, "is 30,000 North Dakota farmers selling through about 500 grain elevators in North Dakota, farmer-owned but discreetly Minneapolis-run . . . into . . . one grain exchange, which in turn sells mostly to six large exporters." The farmers complained that Cargill and other multinational corporations controlled the grain elevators and the Minneapolis Grain Exchange, the largest cash market in the world. Just and his farmer colleagues testified that they often refused to provide the USDA with accurate reports on conditions. That way, they explained, the market wouldn't know what was going on, and the farmers who did know could use their knowledge to make more money.

The farmers from North Dakota wanted to put the multinationals out of business. Just testified that farmers were making efforts to market their grain directly, but "it makes it not only extremely difficult for us, as a small group, to deal in terms of moving it out of the U.S. at the Gulf, or at Duluth, or at Portland, but also for foreign buyers to receive the grain; because . . . Cargill, or Continental, or Bunge may own all the port facilities there."

The subcommittee had intended to continue the debate

with an examination of the other five multinationals. In summer 1976, however, Subcommittee Chair Church became distracted by his abortive run for president. Then the subcommittee and its staff were disappointed by the absence of interest. The press hadn't bothered to cover the hearings, and no one else in Congress seemed especially interested. So the first became the last examination of the multinationals, their role in the marketplace, and the efficiency of the marketplace as determiner of food policy.

Three of the major policy questions raised or implied by these hearings are:

1. *Should farmers replace the marketplace and control price?* The farmers from North Dakota testified that they didn't trust Cargill and the other multinationals because of declining prices. They wanted higher prices and thereby higher incomes. They testified that they were falsifying crop reports and also attempting to take over the export business to increase their income. No senator inquired whether this was in the public interest.

Other farmers did not have to rely on the marketplace; for example, a small number of farmers controlled the price of winter lettuce. Most winter lettuce in cities such as New York, Chicago, and Washington, D.C., came from California, where the Federal Trade Commission charged that lettuce farmers sat around a table and fixed prices. The prices of most fresh vegetables and fruits were determined by farmers or farmers' cooperatives. If a consumer didn't like the price of cranberries, there was no shopping around; cranberries were sold to all stores at the same fixed price.

Whatever its disadvantages, the marketplace protected consumers from paying prices dictated by farmers. The futures markets determined prices for most agricultural products including wheat, corn, soybeans, pork bellies (sliced to become bacon), iced broilers, live cattle, live hogs, frozen orange juice concentrate, and fresh eggs. As their income depended increasingly on exports, farmers benefited from the futures markets that established prices not only domestically but also in the rest of the world. Corn on the Chicago Board of Trade was used to establish prices in Rotterdam, which set the standard throughout Europe. Because European corn could be shipped for delivery at the Chicago Board of Trade, and U.S. corn could be shipped for delivery at foreign exchanges, the United States' productive farmers benefited from the global marketplace and the worldwide competition it encouraged.

Unfortunately farmers also suffered from the market's increased sophistication. Many farmers didn't understand how to reduce risk and protect their incomes by hedging. In 1977 the Commodity Futures Trading Commission said only 5.6 percent of all farmers in the United States with annual sales of more than $10,000 traded in the futures markets. The figures were somewhat better at 13.1 percent for farmers with gross sales of more than $100,000. Because many farmers had not protected themselves, when prices fell they turned to Congress for help, quick to blame the marketplace and the secret international companies that in the exchanges, if nowhere else, were so visible. The farmers asked for government payments. Even on the agriculture committees, Congress knew increasingly less about agriculture and the role of the marketplace, so the farmers' complaints were often sympathetically received.

2. *Is the marketplace honest?* During the 1970s major scandals tarnished the system. They involved charges that various large commercial interests manipulated the futures markets to make unfair profits.

During the Russian grain deal in 1972, the multinational corporations were accused of manipulating futures prices. In February 1973 the *Des Moines Register* reported several irregularities and said, "There are strong indications rigged markets in wheat, eggs, and meats, have cost the public, the small commodity-traders and farmers millions of dollars." Also in 1973 the Chicago Board of Trade suspended trading in soybeans amid charges that four traders allegedly attempted to corner the market. In August 1973 the *Des Moines Register* reported: "The president of a large milling company in Kansas charged . . . that grain export firms have 'cornered' the Kansas City wheat market and are effectively preventing grain from being milled into flour for bread and other domestic products."

Investigators from the Department of Agriculture, charged with policing the major exchanges, demonstrated their ineffectiveness. When the Senate's Permanent Subcommittee on Investigations examined a report on market rigging in 1972, the subcommittee said indignantly that the USDA wasted 1900 staff hours by concentrating its investigation "on the wrong day."

In 1974 Congress created the independent Commodity Futures Trading Commission (CFTC) and gave it considerable authority. For the first time several exchanges, including the New York Sugar Exchange, were regulated.

The CFTC arose because Representative Neal Smith (a Democrat from Iowa) recognized the importance of an honest market; virtually single-handedly, using exposés in the *Des Moines Register* for support, he forced his colleagues to go along. Smith was not a member of the Agriculture Committee, and the Congress that created the CFTC did not realize that by doing so it officially acknowledged the marketplace would continue to dominate food policy.

The CFTC, however, did not generate confidence in its efficiency, either. In 1976, for example, because the CFTC failed to take timely action, the futures market in Maine potatoes collapsed. It ran into several personnel problems. William T. Bagley, the CFTC's first chair, admitted that when President Ford appointed him he didn't know what a futures contract was. Later, after President Carter appointed David G. Gartner to the commission, it was learned that he had accepted for his children stock in a multinational grain-trading company. In 1978 Senator Thomas Eagleton (a Democrat from Missouri) called the CFCT the "most messed up federal agency in the government." The CFTC lacked information about the multinationals, so it could not assure that large, secret, private interests did not exert undue influence on prices. The CFTC's principal virtue was that it had the power and eventually acquired staff with the expertise to prevent blatantly illegal market-rigging.

Meanwhile, during the 1970s, the office of the U.S. Attorney in New Orleans uncovered a major marketplace scandal involving widespread corruption by the multinationals, although few people, even farmers, paid much attention. After more than two years of investigations, in 1976 officials from four of the six multinationals were convicted on charges of mislabeling or misweighing grain and of bribing the government's grain inspectors. Most multinationals had engaged in an industry-wide practice of selling grain that had been improperly graded and weighed.

The government's inspection system was ineffective and antiquated. The so-called inspectors, who received licenses from the USDA, were often employees of private inspecting firms in New Orleans and elsewhere. Some of these firms, in turn, were owned by grain exporters. Thus the inspectors were often paid by the people whose grain was inspected, so there was a tempting opportunity to be corrupt, especially as exports increased. One inspector was convicted of accepting payoffs as high as $5000 to certify that ships were clean and fit to carry grain. Payments were apparently so widespread and so blatant that one check introduced as evidence in the trial noted its purpose as "Gratuities for Grain Surveyor."

It was cheaper to bribe an official than to clean a ship. In June 1975 the *Des Moines Register* reported that wheat intended for human consumption was being loaded into a hold containing oil sludge. The ship had been certified as clean. In August U.S. Attorney Gerald J. Gallinghouse announced indictments from the sale of "at least nine bargeloads" of nonexistent soybeans and corn. Over a three-year period one grain elevator owned by Cook Industries apparently sold 18.6 million bushels of grain more than it received.

"The waterfront is not the Bolshoi Ballet. . . . " an attorney for one New Orleans grain elevator told *The New York Times;* he was commenting on rumors that a contract was out to break both kneecaps of a federal grain inspector who had ignored warnings to keep quiet about bribery and theft. The scandal reached high officers in the hierarchies of multinational corporations. In November 1976 Phillip H. McCall, then president of the Louis Dreyfus Company, which was not implicated, was sentenced to three months in prison for his illegal activities while he was the number-two person at Cook Industries.

An indifferent Congress passed legislation to correct the abuses. Senator Dick Clark and Representative Neal Smith, using exposés in *The New York Times* and the *Des Moines Register* for support, persuaded their colleagues in 1976 to federalize grain inspection and ensure the honesty of the marketing system. Farmers were not interested in the scandal, which broke in late 1974 when their income was at record highs. One staff member on the House Agriculture Committee observed, "You can count on one hand the number of Congressmen who see this as an adrenalin churning issue. There's no mail from angry farmers or consumers so these guys just aren't motivated."

The dirty-grain scandal illustrates how difficult it was for Congress to conduct a debate on food policy. First, the scandal was basically considered boring. Even though James Risser of the *Des Moines Register* received a Pulitzer Prize for his reporting, the public generally did not care. As one USDA official said, "I wouldn't say grain inspection is exciting." In fact reports on the scandal could not answer the readers' basic question, so what? It might be illegal that companies were selling Number 2 yellow corn that had too many broken kernels, or were misweighing grain to be shipped abroad, but it was difficult to say why the American consumer should care.

Eventually the people who had suffered directly were identified in a general way. Much of the misweighed grain had been sent to underdeveloped countries, which did not have facilities to check the weights and discover that they had received less than they bought. The probable consequence was that the poor did not have enough to eat during acute shortages.

Second, the scandal pointed out that farmers and their organizations had a limited ability to identify their own interests. This scandal should have been a bread-and-butter issue for farmers. Since their income depended heavily on exports, it was critical to them that the U.S. maintain a reputation for honestly selling quality grain. Otherwise when the shortage ended and foreign buyers had a choice, they would buy elsewhere.

Instead farmers concentrated on what they did best— producing. They ignored the fact that without government regulation over agriculture, their income depended on the marketplace.

Third, the scandal pointed out the policy problems presented by the multinational corporations' lack of accountability. From the perspective of the multinationals who participated in corruption—and even those who didn't—the scandal was relatively trivial, because they didn't suffer if foreign purchasers disgusted by U.S. products chose, say, Argentinean grain. They handled most of the world's grain, so they benefited no matter which grain was shipped. For them the scandal was over prevailing custom in the U.S.; since it was customary to bribe U.S. inspectors, they did not hold themselves responsible for adhering to standards of honesty that the government had been unwilling to maintain.

Finally, the scandal illustrated Congress's reactive nature. Congress has rarely been able to identify major policy problems in advance and to avoid them. More often it corrects an abuse that is widely perceived as needing correction. In this instance neither the public nor the farmers who were directly affected cared. The agriculture committees were largely indifferent. This time around, Congress acted because there was no significant opposition. Dick Clark and Neal Smith shamed their colleagues into recognizing that this issue had long-term consequences, but they were not able to lead either house in a more comprehensive debate on the nature of U.S. agricultural policy.

3. *Do the multinationals serve the public's interest?* The multinationals' skills at using futures and cash markets, their ability to control transportation from domestic farms to foreign countries, and the intense competition among them caused grain to move quickly and efficiently from one end of the world to the other. Their skill opened up and developed new markets for American farmers and fed the world's hungry, as long as the hungry had money or had governments that had or could borrow money. Attempts by farmers to act as exporters, competing with the multinationals, have generally not been successful, at least in part because what the multinationals do is highly specialized, and they are good at it.

In *Global Reach* Robert J. Barnet and Ronald Muller explain that they dislike using "multinational" to describe the "global" companies changing the way the world does business. "Multinational" implies that foreign operations are simply international branches of a home office. Rather, they say, "The power of the global corporation derives from its unique capacity to use finance, technology and advanced marketing skills to integrate production on a worldwide scale and thus to realize the ancient capitalist dream of One Great Market. This cosmopolitan vision stands as a direct challenge to traditional nationalism."

By 1976 the multinationals' indifference to national goals appeared to work for the United States' interests. Given the isolationist tradition of American agriculture, which Earl Butz first began to shatter in 1972, and Congress's slow reaction to farm-trade issues, without the multinationals the U.S. grain-export trade would certainly have developed more slowly. The multinationals also had developed sophisticated skills to operate within the economic and political conditions of both communist countries and the developing world, which served American interests. Even their ability to ignore this country's embargoes may have worked to our advantage by making the embargoes less effective than intended and thus less able to damage foreign markets.

In 1975 representatives Fred Richmond (a Democrat from New York) and James Weaver (a Democrat from Oregon) introduced legislation to nationalize the grain-trading companies. Although Congress never considered the question seriously, the bill's existence showed how frustrated people were who believed that a country should have control over its own food policy. At the time, however, national trading companies were proving themselves ineffective in Canada and Australia, where the multinationals were being used to make trade more competitive. Nor did the U.S. government demonstrate that it would be more efficient, less corrupt, and more attuned to the public interest than the multinationals, with their indifference to national concerns. The government continued to lack basic information about how agriculture worked and who the major decision-makers were, and Congress was unwilling to develop such information, as the Church subcommittee demonstrated by failing to continue its hearings.

For the government to make intelligent decisions about food policy, it would need to learn something about the subject. In the meantime the marketplace continued to tell farmers what to plant, and it was certainly more qualified to do so than the government.

---

1. "The marketplace," "the futures market," and "the commodities market" are used interchangeably. Specifically "the marketplace" refers to the whole market system, of which the futures markets are only a part, albeit the most significant. "The futures market" refers to the futures exchanges (pits) at the Chicago Board of Trade and elsewhere. Since the futures markets involve speculation on the future price of such commodities as corn, cocoa, and pork bellies, they are also called "commodities markets." A distinction between "futures markets" and "cash markets" is necessary. At a futures market the commodity itself is not traded. That is what the cash market is for. As this chapter develops, it is hoped that the purpose and function of these markets will become clearer.

2. Basically anyone who uses a futures market is a speculator. A speculator is someone who hopes to make money by predicting whether the price of a commodity will go up or down. However, the word "speculator" has come to have pejorative connotations. As a result, speculators using the market for hedging—regarded as a financial tool in the food industry and described later in this chapter—sought to make a distinction between themselves and those concerned only with making a profit. Nevertheless when a futures contract is being traded, the market does not care about the intentions of the buyer or seller. The reader is hereby requested to avoid judging speculation as an inherently nasty activity.

3. The description of hedging has been simplified. A farmer who in September wanted to protect the price for the following September would more likely trade in more recent contracts—such as May's—then cancel out the position and go back into the market. The aim would still be to protect the price in September, and the farmer could simply

hold on to September contracts for about a year. But by using contracts with closer delivery dates the farmer could avoid fluctuations in prices over the longer period, which could involve annoying margin calls (calls from the broker to increase the deposit the farmer gives as a credit guarantee).

Also, hedging can be used in a more sophisticated manner. Thomas A. Hieronymus, author of the authoritative *Economics of Futures Trading*, says flatly that hedging is not insurance. He defines it as "risk shifting" used to "maximize profits." The distinction seems like a quibble, but his point about the sophistication of the marketplace is worth noting. Hieronymus says, "Hedging is an intricate activity, requiring substantial knowledge and operational skills." He explains that the purpose is "to shift the risks of price level changes. . . . The game that hedgers play is one anticipating changes in price relationships, implementing their expectations with equal or opposite positions in cash and futures, and profiting as they are correct and losing as they are wrong."

Chapter Eight

The Power of Agricultural Labor

> Money . . . all is money. All human relationships
> must be purchased with money. If you have no
> money, men won't care for you, women won't love
> you . . . and how right they are, after all! For,
> moneyless you are unlovable.
>
> —*Keep the Aspidistra Flying*
> by George Orwell

The basic premise of capital-intensive agriculture is that labor is expensive. If it weren't there would have been no need to create elaborate farm machinery in the first place.

There were many reasons why the public generally did not realize that reliable and efficient agricultural labor was becoming increasingly valuable. The big agricultural news for consumers throughout the 1970s was that the cost was skyrocketing. Costs rose because America learned the true worth of the complex agricultural system, such as California's Imperial Valley, which we had created and maintained at great governmental expense. Discovering that the world's supply of farmland and other basic resources was limited had shown that the United States' ability to produce high yields of crops was extremely valuable. At the same time the government was getting rid of regulations that no longer worked to keep consumers' food costs artificially low.

In addition, over the previous two decades, the government had slowly changed its regulations and general approach toward agricultural labor, which had formerly subsidized farmers by keeping wages down. When the costs of labor, petroleum, and other resources needed to run a modern farm could no longer remain artificially low, their rise helped raise food costs. Therefore while the skills needed to run a capital-intensive farm became dramatically more complex, governmental subsidies stopped keeping inefficient operations in business. An increasingly critical element in farm efficiency was labor relations.

Large corporate-like farms were discovering that reliable agricultural labor was becoming more scarce, and if a farm wanted to make a profit, it had to attract and retain efficient employees by paying them adequately. Ironically it was Cesar Chavez, even though his rhetoric opposed the overall structure, who first demonstrated how farmworkers could benefit from this large, capital-intensive farming. He also demonstrated that by improving the farmworkers' condition, corporate-like agriculture became more efficient and profitable.

In 1970 Cesar Chavez succeeded in doing what had never been done before. He forced farmers to sign union contracts with their fieldworkers. Chavez achieved this first success by concentrating on a clear and well-defined objective within the specific, highly concentrated industry producing table grapes. Virtually all table grapes produced in the U.S. came from California. About 30 percent were grown in the neighborhood of Delano, a small town in the southern San Joaquin Valley, the principal agricultural valley in the state. Virtually all the rest were grown either a short ride north of Delano or about 260 miles southeast in the Coachella Valley.

Laborers did both unskilled harvest work and year-long semi-skilled tasks such as grafting, pruning, tying, and thinning plants, and maintaining irrigation ditches. As a result

Delano and its neighboring towns had a large population of farmworkers who the table-grape industry employed fulltime or nearly fulltime. For farmworkers they were relatively well paid; in 1965 growers had been forced to raise wages rather than delay harvesting their crop. But Chavez's objective was not to win higher wages. Rather, he saw the opportunity for workers to win union recognition and thereby gain significant control over their working conditions.

Chavez once explained, "I always have had, and I guess I always will have, a firm belief that if you muster enough power, you can move things, but it's all on the basis of power. Now I seldom like to see my opponent unless I have some power over him." In 1962 he formed the National Farm Workers Association, later called the United Farmworkers Union (UFW), to compete with the attempts of both the Teamsters Union and AFL-CIO President George Meany to organize farmworkers. But Chavez's power was theoretical. He had to convince table-grape workers to unite behind him and force the growers to recognize his union. Then his union could provide growers a stable and efficient work force. Later Meany gave up his own effort and allowed Chavez's union to become an AFL-CIO affiliate.

Traditionally the problem in organizing agricultural workers was transience. For example even if harvesters agreed to organize, they might well leave the area or farm employment by the end of the season. Thus it was critical to Chavez that the table-grape industry have a significant number of fulltime workers whose continued employment contributed to the health of the industry. The growers might replace their current farmworkers with others, but Chavez needed to demonstrate that doing it would be more expensive in the long run than recognizing his union.

Chavez's strong ethnic identification was essential to establishing his leadership. Most workers in the table-grape industry, and most California farmworkers generally, were

of Mexican origin. A vast majority were legal residents in
the U.S., and many were citizens whose families had been
in this country for a generation or more. Chavez's grand-
father brought his family across the Mexican border when
his son, Chavez's father, was two years old. Cesar was born
in Yuma County, Arizona, just east of California's Imperial
Valley. "Our family farm was started three years before
Arizona became a state," Chavez said. "Yet, sometimes I
get crank letters . . . telling me to 'go back' to Mexico!"

In the agricultural valleys of California, Mexican-
Americans, especially, suffered from discriminatory treatment comparable to what blacks endured in the South in
Jim Crow days. In farming communities, Anglos and
Chicanos were two distinct and unequal classes separated
by barriers of language, ethnicity, and mutual hostility.
White growers hired Mexican-Americans and controlled
the local power structure. Routine identity-card checks were
one of a series of ways Chicanos were harrassed and reminded
of their place.

Chavez understood viscerally, as only experience can
teach, the shared discrimination that bound the Chicano
community together. He once described an incident from
childhood when he was in California's Imperial Valley: "We
went this one time to a diner; it had a sign on the door
'White Trade Only' but we went in anyway. We had heard
they had these big hamburgers, and we wanted one. There
was a blonde, blue-eyed girl behind the counter—a beauty.

"She asked what we wanted—real tough, you know?—
and when we ordered a hamburger, she said, 'We don't sell
to Mexicans,' and she laughed when she said it. She en-
joyed doing that, laughing at us. We went out, but I was
really mad, enraged. It had to do with my manhood."

Chavez used this shared discrimination to solidify
Mexican-Americans behind him. He also attracted support
from people outside California farm communities who
found such discrimination abhorrent. He used it to attract

attention. During the grape strike Sergeant Gerald Dodd, the sheriff of Kern County, banned the use of the Spanish word for strike—*huelga*—on picket lines. Sergeant Dodd said it was legal to say "strike" on a Kern County picket line, but not "huelga," which was not an "American" word and would incite violence. Chavez saw that Sergeant Dodd had given him a valuable opportunity. He invited clergy-people from various faiths to join him on a picket line, so television cameras and reporters recorded the local sheriff arresting the clergy for speaking Spanish.

Chavez successfully combined ethnic identification with a strong religious base. Many table-grape workers were Filipinos, and like the Chicanos they had strong ties to the Roman Catholic Church. In fact the grape strike began in 1965 when a group of Filipino workers forced Chavez's hand, requiring him to join their strike, which he felt was premature.

Chavez used the church to unite farmworkers by making the Mass a central event in rallies and meetings as a way to sustain morale. He invited priests and nuns to marches and other activities where crosses and other religious symbols were prominently displayed. Receiving church support for his tactic of nonviolence, Chavez reminded audiences that Jesus had preached love for his enemies.

Given the context of the Anglos' power structure, nonviolence was the only effective tactic he had. Had he encouraged workers to damage the fragile grapes, one area where growers were especially vulnerable, or to commit other acts of violence, he would have been destroyed. Instead nonviolence required his farmworker supporters to accept his authority. It put the growers at a severe disadvantage because he could publicize their acts of violence or repression to further his objectives. Nonviolence as practiced by a poor, deeply religious Mexican-American fighting against a powerful, racist power structure attracted support throughout the country.

In 1968 a well-publicized 25-day fast united a coalition of farmworkers' organizations behind Chavez. He explained that he was fasting because tempers were frayed by the three-year-old grape strike and boycott, which were having little success. Afraid of violence in the movement, he announced that he had stopped eating as a way of forcing his followers to change their behavior. He ended the fast during an open-air Mass at which a makeshift altar was placed on a flatbed truck. Robert Kennedy, who was in the process of becoming a presidential candidate, flew into Delano for the event. "I remember the TV people were there," Chavez told his biographer Jacques Levy, "and one cameraman couldn't get in while Kennedy was giving me a piece of bread. When he finally did, he told Kennedy, 'This is probably the most ridiculous request I have ever made. Could you give him a piece of bread again?'"

Chavez knew that the table-grape industry depended on a sophisticated marketing system over which it had little control. By boycotting grapes, he hit the growers at their most vulnerable point—the supermarket. If no one buys table grapes, they rot on the shelf. For supporters the boycott was simple and painless; shoppers had little difficulty identifying what they were asked to boycott, and since the fruit was a luxury item, doing without was no hardship. The effort attracted a coalition of urban groups including labor, student, religious, and ethnic organizations. Every liberal politician in the country let it be known that he or she personally was boycotting grapes. The boycott was effective despite the Nixon administration's attempt to dilute it by making large purchases for U.S. troops.

His strike activities in farm communities reminded urban supporters why they were boycotting, and Chavez realized that without the boycott he could not succeed. He could not win by simply withholding labor for long periods of time the way urban unions won. If necessary the growers could find other workers. He did not discourage farmworkers from working for the growers they were striking, because he recognized that the workers could not do without the income. At times strike activity simply consisted of picketing one field, requiring supporters to withhold work from that field but permitting them to work elsewhere, even for the same grower.

The boycott's objective was to force growers to recognize Chavez's union and negotiate with it. The growers finally did so in 1970 both because they could no longer afford the short- and long-term damage to their markets, and because Chavez had clearly established his leadership and could represent the workers to negotiate and to supply a stable work force.

By 1972, the first full year of Earl Butz's tenure as secretary of agriculture, Cesar Chavez was at the height of his power as a labor-union leader. He had signed contracts representing farmworkers with such corporate giants as Tenneco, United Brands, Purex, Heublein, and Coca-Cola. His union represented workers in California, Florida, and other states, controlling a large part of the country's strawberry, lettuce, and other fruit and vegetable crops. Sixty thousand fieldworkers with negotiated contracts were paying dues to Chavez's union.

Victory meant Chavez had to change his image. He was no longer an outsider arguing against agribusiness and building the public's outrage against the plight of agricultural workers. He led a union that was an integral part of the agricultural industry. He knew being an insider had different rules, but he seemed unable to apply his own wisdom. He devoted little attention to the day-to-day problems of administration, instead continuing to reach out to the coalition of liberal urban supporters who had been encouraged to boycott grapes because he had effectively portrayed his strike as part of the migrant workers' struggle against exploitation.

But the vast majority of the UFW membership was not

migrant, so the talk about the tradition of migrant misery as described in *The Grapes of Wrath* and Edward R. Murrow's "Harvest of Shame" did not apply to his union's members. Although such rhetoric had helped gain recognition for the union, it was no longer appropriate. Rather than abandon it and concentrate on running a union, however, he tried to turn the union into a broad-purpose movement to change society. As a result Chavez gave the Teamsters the opportunity to steal his union away from him.

The emotion-laden tradition Chavez evoked was migrant misery, which frequently was at odds with how agricultural work in the U.S. was actually performed.

In the 1970s the people who kept track of the country's migrant agricultural workers spoke of three separate routes called "streams". Migrants from Belle Glade and other rural communities in the south-central part of Florida traveled through the Atlantic Coast states as far north as New England. From Texas, primarily from communities in the Rio Grande Valley such as Harlinger, migrants traveled north and west to the central, mountain, and northwestern states. From the Imperial Valley, migrants traveled the length of California and into Oregon, Washington, and Idaho.

With some regional variations, migrants traveled north during the summer, finding seasonal harvesting and other fieldwork, and returned to their home communities in winter to work on local crops. Some migrants with no home were perpetually on the road.

Generally the migrants' legal employer was a crew leader, who contracted with local farmers to pick a field at a given rate, and who then paid the workers directly. The crew leader arranged for transportation, buses or an automobile caravan, and for housing, food, and other supplies. Some crew leaders had considerable power over their workers, dominating every aspect of their lives. Because the crew leaders paid the workers and also charged for their own services, there was potential for abuse. Some migrants found themselves in a perpetual state of indebtedness, unable to work off their debt to the crew leader and thus unable to stop working. Some were easy targets because they were illiterate, knew no other way of life, and were afraid to complain about working conditions.

Although this description of crew leaders and the migrant streams is an oversimplification, it is partially accurate. There were migrants in the 1970s who traveled thousands of miles each year harvesting fruits and vegetables, weeding sugar beets, and doing other agricultural work. Some were exploited shamelessly. But most experts agreed that the significance of migrants to the country's overall agricultural work force was marginal.

Figures on the number of migrants in the United States has been a subject of dispute because migrants move and are difficult to count, because it is easier to exploit workers who are not counted, and also because figures are used to obtain funds for social programs. The best available figures are from USDA's respected publication *The Hired Farm Working Force,* the only continuing series measuring farm migrancy. In 1976 there were 2.8 million persons 14 years of age and over who did hired farmwork sometime during the year. Two hundred thirteen thousand of them were defined as migrants; they "traveled across county lines from their usual place of residence to stay overnight and do hired farm work." A group of economists who analyzed this information estimated that migrants "may not do as much as 3 percent of all . . . work in the nation's farming."

By 1976 the number of migrants had been decreasing for decades, as they and their families settled down, and the streams were "drying up." Not only were fewer people migrating, but those who did spent less time on the road, and most no longer conformed to the traditional image.

Young workers were being encouraged to join crews. Sixty percent of migrants were under 25; 33 percent were students; 72 percent were males, and 57 percent were white. The traditional migrant families, whose very old and very young members worked in the fields, were disappearing. It was still possible to find crew leaders and others ruthlessly exploiting migrant families, but they were only a small percentage of the dwindling migrant labor force.

Nevertheless, the public still carried an underlying assumption that migrants did a lot of the work and that they and farmworkers in general were badly exploited. This perception was based on two distinct and separate events. The first was the Great Depression, when the farmworkers' problems were part of the larger economic disaster affecting the entire farm community. In the 1930s nearly everyone on farms suffered—the whole farming family, the fulltime farm hand, the seasonal workers, and the migrant. When farmers went out of business they often became farmworkers. The most lasting and graphic representation of farmworkers' powerlessness during that period is in John Steinbeck's *The Grapes of Wrath*, which farmworkers' advocates cited throughout the 1960s and '70s even in legal briefs as a classic description of migrants' problems. Steinbeck's heroes were Oklahoma farmers forced off the land by low prices and encouraged to migrate to California by deliberately deceptive reports of high wages. Their enemies were the large corporate-like farmers and the collapse of the farm economy, which depressed wages and living conditions for everyone.

The second event was the combination of dramatic advances in and widespread application of mechanization in the 1960s and the poverty that accompanied it in some rural communities. The most significant revelation of this poverty took place on April 11, 1967, when the Senate Subcommittee on Employment, Manpower, and Poverty took a field trip outside Jackson, Mississippi. The subcommittee was holding routine oversight hearings on War on Poverty programs. Committee member Robert Kennedy, then senator from New York, recommended the trip at the private urging of Martin Luther King, Jr., who knew the widespread mechanization of cotton had put fieldworkers out of work. In 1949 less than 10 percent of the crop had been harvested by machine; by 1969 the figure was at least 95 percent. Because the largely black unemployed fieldworkers had no place to go, no money or transportation to leave, and were ineligible for food stamps, welfare, or other government assistance, some were starving to death in rural communities.

King hoped that if senators saw U.S. citizens starving, they would demand that the country's agricultural surpluses be used to feed them. That is exactly what happened. The official discovery of hunger in the U.S. shocked the subcommittee. Senator George Murphy, a conservative Republican from California, said, "I didn't know that we were going to be dealing with the situation of starving people and starving youngsters." The subcommittee unanimously told the president that the situation required emergency action, and suddenly hunger in the U.S. became a major political issue, eventually resulting in sweeping changes in the food-stamp and other food programs.

The discovery also affected how the public perceived the problems of farmworkers who—especially migrants—were considered the least powerful group in society. Indeed many were powerless, especially as advances in mechanization forced them to compete among themselves for a dwindling number of low-paying jobs. Edward R. Murrow helped to define this image of powerlessness in his classic television documentary "Harvest of Shame."

Broadcast on Thanksgiving Day 1960, the CBS documentary showed crew leaders selecting men, women, and children for the day's work. Murrow assured viewers that, contrary to appearances, this was the United States and not South Africa, and the workers were U.S. citizens and not slaves. Beginning in Belle Glade, Florida, Murrow followed the migrant stream. His report, he said, "has to do with the men, women, and children who harvest the crops in this country of ours, the best-fed nation on earth. These are the forgotten people; the underprotected; the underclothed; the underfed. We present this report on Thanksgiving because were it not for the labor of the people you are going to meet, you might not starve, but your table would not be laden with luxuries that we have all come to regard as essentials. We should like you to meet some of your fellow citizens who harvest the food for the best-fed nation on earth."

Murrow's cameras showed the country a farmworker distinctly different from the one described in *The Grapes of Wrath*. One could not imagine these migrants ever becoming farmers even long enough to go bankrupt. Unlike farmworkers in the Depression, who were part of the farm community and suffered along with it, these people were suffering despite the widespread agricultural prosperity around them. The problem was also increasingly outside the public's experience. In the Depression 25 percent of the population lived on farms and could directly evaluate conditions in rural areas and put problems within the larger context of the farm economy; in 1960 fewer than 6 percent lived on farms, and by 1970 only 4.8 percent did. Despite the absence of population in rural areas, however, a large part of the public was appalled by the exploitation and poverty.

Robert Kennedy was one of the first politicians to realize that while the nation prospered, the migrants' poverty and powerlessness had become politically significant. In 1965 an outraged Kennedy, assigned to the apparently obscure Senate Subcommittee on Migratory Labor, told a witness from the Farm Bureau, "This is the first time I have heard you, so perhaps this comes as more of a shock to me; to be opposed to a minium wage, to be opposed to legislation which would limit the use of children between the ages of

10 and 13 for working, to be opposed to collective bargaining completely . . . to oppose all that without some alternative makes the rest of the arguments you have senseless."

The following year Kennedy met Cesar Chavez, who had appeared before the subcommittee to testify that such hearings were useless. He opposed government programs serving farmworkers and said the only effective solution was for farmworkers to solve their own problems. They could do so, he said, by organizing a powerful union. As a consequence of this testimony Kennedy and Chavez formed a strong friendship, which each used for his own political advantage.

In 1970, the same year Chavez forced growers to recognize his union, the Government Printing Office published the *Migrant and Seasonal Farmworker Powerlessness Hearings* in 16 thick volumes. Not only had Robert Kennedy served on the subcommittee, but the chair was Senator Walter Mondale, whose services helped establish his liberal credentials within the Democratic party, which later influenced Jimmy Carter to make him his running mate. During the 1984 election, vice presidential candidate Geraldine Ferraro pointed to Mondale's concern for migrants as proof of the compassion a president should have.

In a novel suggestive of the dramatic potential of the misery, Tom Wicker described a freshman senator who turns his assignment on a migratory labor subcommittee into a springboard for the presidency: "As the slow point-counterpoint of grower and migrant, society and outcast, exploitation and dependence, continued in the musty old chamber, there came to be just enough drama, just enough moments of passion and truth, with just enough of them frozen in time by the camera, or broadcast indiscriminately by the wonders of radio and television, that like a Broadway show the hearings became a 'hot ticket'. . . . Sometimes those waiting outside for a seat to empty could hear a burst of applause or the sharp rapping of the gavel, and once the angry shouts of a grape man from the Imperial Valley could be heard clearly in the corridor. Adam Locklear had produced the facts on the grape man's illegal importation of wetbacks into virtual slavery."

In 1973 an internal Labor Department report said that because of loopholes in federal and state laws, many migrants had been excluded from such basic employee benefits as worker's compensation, minimum wages, unemployment insurance, Social Security, as well as equal protection under the law. Many had been administratively excluded from food stamps and commodity-distribution programs, public assistance, employment counseling, voting, and civil-rights protection. They often had inadequate housing, inadequate health care, and "inadequate income." They were losing their jobs to legal and illegal aliens and to increased mechanization. Most of the income of migrant agricultural workers, the report noted, came from nonagricultural work.

Because of the continuous and dramatic attention on migrants, throughout the 1960s and '70s the government created laws and programs to solve their problems. In 1976 the Department of Labor spent more than $73 million for migrants, primarily on job-training programs. The Department of Health, Education, and Welfare spent $150 million on migrants' education and $30 million on their health. The Department of Agriculture spent $12 million on migrants' housing. The Legal Services Corporation spent $2 million.

As eligibility requirements eased up, migrants also received governmental assistance from programs for the larger public, such as food stamps, welfare, and general job training. They received state and local assistance and were served by several nonprofit organizations funded by foundations, churches, and concerned citizens.

Throughout the 1970s governmental funding for migrants

expanded rapidly as courts forced the executive branch to turn federally subsidized local or experimental social programs into national efforts. Ironically the Nixon administration helped cause this expansion by attempting to reduce social spending. Not only did Nixon, Butz, and others in the administration appear insensitive to the poor and powerless, but they used questionable tactics including impounding funds already approved by Congress, a device that was ruled unconstitutional. The administration generated so much animosity that it forced federal programs and the nonprofit organizations that they supported and that supported them in return to unite against the common enemy and effectively lobby a receptive Democratic Congress.

This conflict between the president and Congress caused considerable inefficiency and distracted programs and organizations from serving migrants. Even when the migrants' lobby privately agreed that a program was poorly run, criticism was muted. Given the seige mentality of the time, attempts to require accountability were regarded as attacks on the poor. As a result the programs evolved into a confused hodgepodge and even if the government had wanted to develop a coherent strategy for solving migrants' problems, it would have been unable to do so. In 1974, for example, five federal agencies were using six separate definitions of *migrant* to determine eligibility for programs. Multiple definitions and incomplete statistics made it difficult to locate migrants, identify their needs, and evaluate whether a program was effective.

The basic premise behind the programs was that the migrants' problems were caused by their way of life. The first objective was to encourage them to stop traveling. If they stayed in one place, the government could provide them with adequate housing, health services, food, and other assistance. The second objective was to help them obtain fulltime employment, primarily in nonagricultural jobs that were better paying and more secure. Therefore the Labor

Department trained migrants to be welders and mechanics. The children were given special educational programs to bring them up to the level of other students so they could learn their way out of the migrant stream and agricultural employment.

As an interim measure farmworkers' advocates wanted to improve working conditions. Frequently the same people who openly praised small farmers and spoke contemptuously of agribusiness were responsible for closing exemptions that applied to small farmers. Corporate farmers had to pay a minimum wage, although it was lower than the industrial minimum wage, and provide other basic employee benefits. Small farmers were exempted entirely from the minimum wage and were exempted from or evaded laws related to occupational safety and other matters. When the exemptions were closed, several small farmers went out of business, having been subsidized in their marginal farming by low labor costs. Others reduced labor costs by mechanizing more rapidly, reducing employment.

Meanwhile the same advocates who encouraged migrants to look for nonagricultural jobs complained that the USDA's research in mechanization put farmworkers out of work.

As the combined economic conditions and government programs stopped workers from migrating, they were no longer migrants. This change presented a problem for the programs that served them, because their funding was based on the number of migrants they served. Agencies used broad definitions and defined *migrants* as people not currently migrating or doing agricultural work but who had a history of such work or whose families had. At the same time migrant programs began referring to themselves as farmworkers' programs to make all farmworkers synonymous with migrants in the public mind and to make all agricultural labor synonymous with poverty. But a 12-year-old girl from Belle Glade, Florida, who helped her migrant family dig potatoes in Exmore, Virginia, had a very different job from a 36-year-old man driving a 16-row radish harvester in Belle Glade.

The sleight of hand with definitions and statistics, whereby some agencies served millions of "migrants" even though only about 213,000 people did such work on a regular basis, pointed out a fundamental problem within the bureaucracy. The programs assumed that migrants had problems characteristic of their lifestyle that general social-service and poverty programs were unable to solve. But once the people stopped moving and stopped working in agriculture, they were no longer migrants or farmworkers and had needs similar to those of other poor people. There was no cause for a separate set of farmworkers' programs. Some programs duplicated the services of other social agencies. Although occasional examples of exploited migrants came to their attention, the programs had become poverty programs that devoted less and less time and attention to the relative handful of workers remaining in the fields. Nevertheless they continued to regard their function as part of the solution to the "Harvest of Shame" tradition and held onto the 1960s rhetoric.

The federal programs and their associated nonprofit organizations, which had been formed and funded partly as a result of public indignation aroused by Murrow's description of how crops were harvested, realized that their continued existence required that the indignation remain high. Liberal congressmen and foundations that supported the migrants' bureaucracy said they were helping solve the problems of society's most powerless workers. Labor unions, church organizations, and others felt good that they too were working against exploitation. They all benefited from a description of agricultural labor that was no longer accurate. But the public generally did not visit traditional migrants' communities such as Belle Glade, Florida, so it did not realize how much the patterns had changed. The public relied on the "experts" who wanted to keep their programs funded.[1]

Cesar Chavez benefited from the indignation about migrants. The nonprofit groups and even the federal programs gave him considerable direct and indirect assistance, which not only helped make the grape boycott effective, but also forced the government to close off the legal importation of seasonal agricultural workers from Mexico, which was a critical factor in Chavez's success. Unlike the bureaucracy, however, Chavez could not avoid adapting to the changed situation. As the leader of a union providing agricultural labor, he was accountable for measurable progress.

After Chavez won the grape strike in 1970, he announced that his union would replace the crew-leader system with union-run hiring halls. Most of UFW's dues-paying members lived in the community where they worked, and many drove their own cars to the fields. Despite the traditional crew-leader stereotype, for them a crew leader was nothing more than a supervisor. Under Chavez's new and unnecessarily burdensome system, workers were required to report to a hiring hall every morning rather than go directly to work. The system might have worked if the union, no longer poor, had hired competent administrators. But because Chavez didn't replace his volunteer staff, whose primary strength had been to fight with growers, with a professional one, the hiring hall created an administrative nightmare. Growers had to wait as long as two days for workers who were also waiting in the hiring hall wanting to work. Chavez said the workers ran his union, and they would sort things out.

Because Chavez was unable to do everything at once, he neglected significant problems such as procedures at the hiring halls to issue a stream of memoranda on letterhead reading "OFFICE OF THE PRESIDENT," to take care of petty details, and to undercut the authority of competent members of his administration. In *Chavez and the Farm Workers* Ron Taylor described Chavez "helping out the accounting department" by adding up checks that had been incorrectly counted. Taylor noted, "Chavez has been trying to delegate more and more authority, but in this effort he is clearly a man at odds with himself."

In 1973 Jack Quiggly, Chavez's business manager, quit. Quiggly had argued, "If you spend some money on adult staff who have some experience and you have administrators to run the offices and the field offices, you pay them modest salaries, it would pay off in better relations with the growers, better administration of the contracts. . . . It's not a big deal. Remove the hassle. Then the Teamsters can't come in and take over because the United Farm Workers is known for the radical kids that it puts into jobs that pay $5 a week."

Larry Iltliong, the Filipino leader whose workers precipitated the 1965 grape strike, resigned from the UFW because of the needless bureaucratic procedures. "We in the top echelon of the organization," he said, "make too many of the rules and we change the rules so very quickly that the workers themselves don't understand what the hell is going on."

Chavez had forced the growers to realize that they could not prevent unionization. But after they signed contracts with him, he did not work with them or allay their fears that his union would interfere with their business. Instead he said, "Nothing short of radical change is going to have any impact on our lives and our problems." His continual talk of changing "the system" and "radical change" made growers increasingly uneasy. Before long they decided that if there had to be a union, it might as well be one they could live with. Produce drivers in California had been working under Teamster contracts for years, and the Teamsters had tried to organize field workers with little success. Chavez had proven that victory was possible, however, and when the Teamsters saw Chavez was vulnerable, they seized their chance.

When the Teamsters took over Chavez's contracts, they reportedly colluded with growers to destroy the UFW. Their original contracts were reportedly "sweetheart" deals arranged by a white union hierarchy that believed Mexican workers were incapable of making their own decisions. Some people also speculate that the Nixon administration pressured Teamster President Frank Fitzsimmons to break his hands-off agreement with the AFL-CIO's President George Meany.

By 1974, after the Teamsters stepped into the power vacuum Chavez had created, one estimate put the UFW's membership at fewer than 5000. Chavez was in danger of having his eleven remaining contracts wrested from him, and it looked as if he might become the leader of a union with no dues-paying members in California.

Meanwhile the Teamsters solidified their base. They removed their goons from the fields and paid dedicated Chicano organizers $200 a week. By 1976 Teamster leaders were consulting directly with the workers. The Teamsters had better health-insurance plans than the UFW, settled grievances more efficiently, and negotiated better contracts. They saw no need to replace the crew-leader system and were building a strong farmworkers' union. They already controlled trucks, warehouses, terminal stations, even supermarkets. Growers were subject not only to pressure at the marketplace, as Chavez's boycott established, but the Teamsters were demonstrating they were also vulnerable transporting goods to market. Roy Mendoza, the Teamsters' assistant director for organizing farm labor, observed, "The difference between our union and the UFW is that we're a labor union. We care about wages and Chavez wants to change the whole system."

Chavez, whose beatific smile, hunger strikes, and friendship with Bobby Kennedy made him a cultural hero of the late 1960s, was still an object of hero worship. The feeling about him was perhaps best expressed in 1976 by Representative Ron Dellums (a Democrat from California), who confessed that he had never met Martin Luther King, Jr. "When I met Cesar for the first time," Dellums said, "I felt the same way about him that I thought I would have felt if I had met Martin Luther King." Dellums also said that he owed his election to Congress to Chavez's active campaigning in his district, which helped carry the critical Chicano vote.

Chavez's supporters were outraged at any critical evaluation of the man or his union. In September 1974 *The New York Times Magazine* published "Is Chavez Beaten?" by Withrop Griffith. Griffith said that after a heroic struggle, the UFW had difficulty administering the contracts it had won. The union had attempted too many reforms too quickly, and he cited the hiring-hall system. Although such problems are understandable in a fledgling union unused to power, Griffith observed that the Teamsters and the growers collusively took advantage of the situation. Having obtained the contracts, however, the Teamsters were trying to hold on to their newly acquired membership, he said, and they appeared to have the experience and the resources to serve the farmworkers. Although many farmworkers greatly admired Chavez, they were signing with the Teamsters because they did not believe the UFW's idealism and attempts at social reform could help them as much as working under a good union contract that was strongly enforced. Griffith concluded by pointing out that Chavez had been through hard times before, and that it was too early to tell just who would win.

Richard E. Chavez, Cesar's brother and a member of the UFW's executive board, called the article a "racist-filled piece of garbage." He asked how the *Times* could allow it to appear in print. "Mr. Griffith goes to great pains, paragraph after paragraph, to degrade and subvert the

United Farm Workers Union and its members, making its leadership and officers appear to be little less than clowns, while coming back, time after time, to praise the lilywhite growers, and the Teamsters for their intelligence, capabilities and power."

Had farmworkers been protected in 1973 by arbitration procedures guaranteed to other Americans through the National Labor Relations Board (NLRB), an election would have been held; the workers would have chosen the UFW — the "Chavistas" as the movement was popularly called — and the Teamsters would have lost in their attempt to steal field workers from another union. But farmworkers were excluded from NLRB protection, an exclusion Chavez opposed at the time but later supported. By late 1974 Chavez increasingly spoke of his role as the head of a social movement, and the UFW referred to itself as "La Causa" ("The Movement"). Rather than concentrate on servicing his handful of remaining contracts and strengthening his union, he became involved with increasingly sophisticated political activities and reached out toward the television cameras and the urban voters. He gambled that by playing politics, he could create a state law to mandate the farmworkers' elections the UFW so desperately needed. Mandatory elections would force field workers to choose between their emotional attachments — most admired Chavez as a cultural and religious leader — and their pocketbooks. The quicker elections were held, the more likely Chavez was to win. Chavez argued that employee benefits under Teamster contracts were only temporary until the Teamster-grower conspiracy succeeded in defeating La Causa.

The gamble paid off. In November 1974 Jerry Brown was elected governor by a narrow margin. Brown, who had marched with Chavez at demonstrations and had helped the UFW when he was California's secretary of state, had sought Chavez's support during the general election. Mexican-Americans were the largest minority in the state, and although most of them lived in urban areas, they respected Chavez as a cultural hero. That respect translated into enough votes that when Brown won the election, he felt Chavez held his large IOU.

In 1975 Brown paid off by creating the Agricultural Labor Relations Act (ALRA) and got considerable political benefit from doing so. In fact when Brown became a presidential candidate in 1976, *The Washington Post* called the ALRA the "outstanding achievement" of his administration. In what was described as a "virtuoso performance" to "end farm strife in California," Brown held a series of 'round-the-clock bargaining sessions in his office. One grower complained, "For some reason, the Governor likes to work at three in the morning." In May 1975 what one Sacramento lobbyist called "the three biggies of agribusiness" — the Farm Bureau, the Agriculture Council of California, and the Agriculture Committee of the State Chamber of Commerce — as well as representatives of the UFW and Governor Brown reached an acceptable compromise. The governor, using a speaker phone, called Cesar Chavez at his headquarters and asked, "Can we count on your support?" To the applause of the major farm groups, Chavez said, "Very, very definitely."

Labor strife had been creating bad public relations for California agriculture, and many people were afraid the Teamsters were becoming too powerful just as contracts were coming up for renewal. One farm group spokesperson explained, "I think most growers are disillusioned with the Teamsters. . . . [S]ome growers recently had cars smashed up and sprinkler heads cut off." The Teamsters would have preferred no law, but they had to accept what Chavez, the governor, and the growers had forced upon them.

Brown promised to appoint an impartial five-member Agricultural Labor Relations Board (ALRB), but four of the appointees were regarded as pro-labor, and three were closely identified with Chavez. One, LeRoy Chatfield, had even worked on Chavez's personal staff. (Later Chatfield resigned from the ALRB to help run Brown's presidential campaign.)

Through the summer of '75 and into '76, elections were conducted on individual farms. Workers had the option of choosing the UFW, the Teamsters, or no union representation at all. The UFW won 54 percent of the elections, but it was clear that field workers were willingly choosing the Teamsters. Chavez regarded the Teamster victories as an attack on his credibility; he had consistently maintained that the Teamsters were a company union and that if workers were given an honest election, they would throw out the Teamsters.

Since 1973 Chavez's primary attention had not been on organizing of farmworkers to sign their first union contracts, but on winning back the contracts that the Teamsters had taken from him. His boycotts against Gallo wine, lettuce, and other products were intended to force farms with Teamster contracts to hold elections. In March 1976, when the ALRB tally showed the Teamsters were the clear choice of workers on 120 ranches, the San Francisco magazine *Mother Jones* commented, "To many people who had worked for the UFW and supported its boycotts during its battle to be recognized and later against the Teamsters, the fact that the UFW hasn't won virtually all of the elections has been surprising."

In March 1976, at an interview in his union headquarters, Chavez was asked about Teamster charges that he ran a social movement, not a union concerned with bread-and-butter issues. He laughed, "I guess what we have is a bread-and-butter social movement." Then, avoiding discussion on how well the UFW dealt with bread-and-butter issues and the differences between the contracts, Chavez explained the importance of a social movement. "We're going through the same problems that the Italians and the Jews and that other groups from foreign countries went through a hundred years, maybe fifty years ago. I don't think that it is only an economic problem. They are the problems that any immigrant group goes through in the beginning, problems with language and with acceptance."

In 1976 Chavez lived at the UFW headquarters in a small wood-frame house guarded by an attack dog and surrounded by a high chain-link fence. Chavez christened the headquarters, a 300-acre complex in the Tehachapi Mountains, La Paz (The Peaceful Place). A Hollywood movie producer bought the former tuberculosis sanitorium for the union. Marc Grossman, Chavez's press secretary, said, "We are the only union that I know of that owns a mountain." Less than 35 miles from the San Joaquin Valley, the entrance to La Paz warned, "Private property, entry by permission only," and a 24-hour security gate and roving patrols protected the fortress-like headquarters from intrusion. Chavez kept one or the other of his two personal attack dogs, "Huelga" and "Strike," with him at all times. La Paz housed data-processing equipment, industrial art facilities, printing presses capable of producing books, protest-button-making machines, training centers, the union's own insurance company, a trailer park, a fleet of buses, kennels for breeding and training Chavez's German shepherd guard dogs, bee hives, and the union's own telephone system. It had a resident population of about 150.

Chavez surrounded himself with volunteers paid a token $5 a week. Key staff members did not know the answers to such basic questions as: How many dues-paying members does the union have? What is currently being boycotted? Why do Teamster contracts provide for unemployment insurance while those of the UFW do not? If asked, they responded with indignation, as if the reporter were betraying a lack of faith in the asking, and they digressed with descriptions of Chavez's vegetarianism, feats of self-denial, and yoga exercises.

By 1976 it was clear that Chavez had made a comeback.

The victories won because of the Agricultural Labor Relations Act gave him a secure dues-paying membership. Yet he continued to talk like a defeated man. Staff members still received only $5 a week "because we are a poor union." His staff continued to be unprofessional, ineffective, and composed of a surprising number of white liberals who did not speak Spanish and who were supported by their parents or lived on food stamps. Asked about his political power when the governor came to La Paz for long walks with his "friend," Chavez, said, "We are a weak movement." Yet he talked with relish about the "electrifying effect" on rural areas when the Mexicans who were permanent resident aliens became naturalized and voted. "Right now, it is more difficult to influence the decisions on the Delano city council than on the Congress of the United States," he said. Chavez, then 49, talked about being an old man, saying that his goal in life was to win union recognition for farmworkers, a goal he had already achieved.

Chavez was concerned by reports that workers were willingly choosing the Teamsters. Rather than concentrating on strengthening his union, he attacked the very ALRB that had made his return to power possible. In September 1975, less than a month after the Agricultural Labor Relations Act took effect, Chavez sent a long telegram to Governor Brown complaining about the board's administration: "Your law has become one more vehicle with which growers and Teamsters can oppress farmworkers." In October the UFW issued a 63-page "white paper" claiming that "the law is being subverted and sabotaged, and its promise is being turned to ashes." In November Chavez wrote an article for the *Los Angeles Times* entitled "Why the Farm Labor Act Isn't Working."

By February 1976, after holding more than 400 elections in less than five months, and after reporting UFW victories on 193 ranches, the board ran out of money. Jerry Brown had not realized that the first effort of its kind would prove so complicated, that there would be so many challenges and disputes, that translators would have to be provided and ballots printed in the various farmworker languages — Spanish, Arabic, Tagalog (a Filipino language), and Punjabi — and that so many elections would take place in the state's agricultural areas that stretch 550 miles from north to south and 50 to 80 miles from east to west.

When the money ran out the fragile Chavez-grower coalition collapsed, and Chavez found himself supporting the law he had only recently attacked. Meanwhile the growers, joined by a hastily assembled coalition of conservative Democrats, Republicans, and Teamsters, succeeded in blocking Govenor Brown's emergency request for additional funding. The request required a two-thirds vote in the state legislature, and the holdouts wanted the law amended and the board composition revised to be less biased in Chavez's favor. For example Chavez was permitted to continue boycotting growers that sold Teamster-picked grapes and lettuce, which the National Labor Relations Board would not have allowed, even though the ALRA prevented growers from dictating to their workers what union to have.

Brown resisted the changes, and when the legislature failed to come up with the necessary votes, Chavez called it "a day of infamy" and said, "Growers are stabbing farmworkers and the people of California in the back. It is an act of treachery that threatens the peace and progress achieved in five short months under the Agricultural Labor Relations Act." He threatened to "pin agriculture to the wall" and announced a new boycott, which, he said, the *Norwegian* parliament had voted to support. The boycott was intended to force the growers, whom he had identified as the ringleaders in the appropriations fight, in turn to force their legislators to change their votes. It was a boycott of raisins, walnuts, and the products of "the Fresno eight," a group of ranchers the UFW press secretary was unable to identify readily. Chavez was dangerously diluting the effectiveness of the boycott by using it too often for goods that were increasingly difficult to identify. Chavez accused the speaker of the Assembly, who was trying to pass the appropriations measure, of "blackmail" and of conspiring with the Teamsters and the growers when, for practical reasons, he delayed calling a vote.

By July the board was back in operation and fully funded, but Chavez had already collected enough signatures to put on the ballot Proposition 14, a citizens' initiative that would have required state funding for the ALRA. (The initiative process makes it possible for the electorate in California to create law directly.) But the legislature had provided the board's necessary funds, and the initiative would change neither the substance nor the operation of the law. Even so, Chavez regarded the Proposition 14 fight as a test of his leadership. He presented the issue as a choice between the poor, exploited migrants whom he claimed to represent and the Teamster-grower conspirators who were exploiting them.

One UFW poster showed a small girl picking onions and putting them into an empty pesticide can. The poster explained that the child was working at the Garin Company in Mettler, California, that she had been hired by a crew leader, and that she was earning 35 cents for each forty-pound bag of onions she picked. The Garin Company sued, claiming that it didn't farm in Mettler, that it didn't use pesticide cans to hold produce, that it wasn't farming onions on the date described, that it hadn't employed the named crew leader, and that it didn't use child labor.

During the campaign Chavez participated in religious masses and fasts, and his supporters made television commercials. One, designed to show farmworkers as the victims of California's huge corporate agriculture, featured Governor Brown claiming that the petroleum companies were spending huge sums behind the scenes. "They don't put the president of Standard Oil on TV to talk about Proposition 14," Brown said sarcastically, even after a Chavez spokesman admitted, "No oil company has had anything to do with the campaign itself." By supporting the initiative Brown secured the continued allegiance of the liberal community at the same time that he was reducing state services to the indigent and unemployed. Chavez's friendship helped him, and Chavez formally nominated Brown for president on network television at the Democratic convention.

When he was running for president against Ford, Jimmy Carter endorsed the initiative as the price Governor Brown exacted for his questionable "support," even though Carter's strategists were afraid the initiative would cost Carter his natural constituents, "non-urban conservative Democrats." They believed that in a close election, supporting Proposition 14 could very well cost Carter the state and thereby the election—and it nearly did. Carter became president with a small fifty-six-vote electoral margin, and he lost California with its forty-five electoral votes by less than two percentage points. Fewer than 140,000 voters would have changed the outcome. Proposition 14 may have made the difference. *The Los Angeles Times,* a consistent Chavez supporter, said, "Opponents of Proposition 14, including this newspaper, argued essentially that the farm labor statute was not needed. California's current farm labor law is identical in all significant respects with the proposed initiative." The initiative lost by a resounding 1.8 million votes.

Even though both sides in the Proposition 14 fight raised approximately the same amount—more than a million dollars each—Chavez claimed that because the growers had raised money earlier, they reached the media sooner, and that's what cost him the election. In a postmortem he told reporters that it is hard to win when you are poor and outside the power structure, but that his movement would eventually prevail.

Meanwhile the Teamsters had come through the summer with a successful cannery strike. (Fifty percent of all vegetables grown commercially in the United States are canned.) By December Chavez and the Teamsters were holding secret negotiations to end their jurisdictional dispute. Three months later photographs showed Cesar Chavez and Teamster President Frank Fitzsimmons embracing. The UFW had jurisdiction over operations the unions agreed were devoted primarily to farming, so some truck drivers would be represented by the UFW. Chavez would inherit expiring Teamster contracts and a potential force of more than 300,000 workers. The Teamsters retained jurisdiction over canneries and food processing plants.

Chavez later signed a contract with growers formally abandoning his union-hiring-hall position. Under one grape contract the lowest-income workers had a minimum annual income of $7200. Orchard workers' contracts provided minimums of $11,648 a year.

It was natural that Chavez's success began in California, the nation's richest agricultural state, where 25 percent of the country's food was produced. From the perspective of a union leader, one of California's advantages was that it needed agricultural workers year-round. Because of its mild climate and fertile soil, much of the farmland yielded two or three crops a year, and the valleys were so fertile they could grow virtually anything commercially. In one county alone some 200 crops from wheat to oranges were in production. California's farmers had to employ a large fulltime labor force.

The employment situation on California's large corporate farms was therefore distinctly different from what happened in the rest of the country. Most farm work was done by the farmer's whole family, and hired workers were only a fraction of the labor force. In 1976 about 4.4 million people did farm work, and nearly 3 million were the farmers and their families. Less than 1.4 million were hired fulltime, and only 213,000 were migrants. In Iowa, the nation's second-richest agricultural state, more than 84 percent of the labor force were farmers and their families. In California, on the other hand, less than 23 percent were farmers; the rest were hired workers. In Iowa the demand for hired help jumped from 8.3 percent of the farm labor force to a high of 24.3 percent during the harvest. But in California it made good business sense to increase the size of one's fulltime payroll, encouraging employees to make a career out of farmwork by providing good wages and fringe benefits. This strategy reduced the expensive problems of not having enough available personpower during critical times, and of paying for low productivity caused by high turnover. Unlike the rest of the country, California needed more farmworkers despite new labor-saving machines such as harvesters with electronic scanners that told when tomatoes were ready for harvest. Not only were hired workers replacing family members, who were leaving the farm, but throughout the 1970s farmland was being created. In 1972 California had 8 million irrigated acres, twice as many as in 1939, and it expected to have 10 million irrigated acres by 1986. More land required more workers. In 1974 287,000 people worked on the state's farms, an increase of 5100 over 1973 and of 7500 over 1972. Because machinery was more advanced, not only were more workers needed, but they had to be more skilled.

The multinational companies such as United Brands and Tenneco, which respectively farmed 22,000 acres and 1.4 million acres in California and Arizona, had considerable experience maintaining large payrolls and dealing with labor unions. Although they preferred that their workers not have a union, they certainly did not share the attitude of the Arizona farmer who told *The Yuma Daily Sun* that he would rather burn his fields than "deal with Cesar Chavez's union." Many of California's corporate-like farmers recognized that a union could serve them in ways they could not serve themselves. A union, especially Chavez's United Farm Workers, which provided its members with an ethnic bond, could offer an efficient and stable work force because union members felt they were part of an organization concerned with their interests. The union bargained with the employers for higher wages, handled grievances, administered benefits, and protected job security. In return the members were obliged to go to the union if they had a problem, rather than just quit.

During the 1960s and 1970s the increased role of both legal and illegal aliens in the farm labor force had become a major issue. For Mexicans and other aliens agricultural work was their entrée to the benefits American society offered, so they did work U.S. citizens were increasingly unwilling to do.

This change from domestic to alien labor was especially apparent in Belle Glade, Florida, one of the three traditional home-base communities for the migrant streams. Each year growers flew more than 8500 Jamaicans into the area, even though farmworkers already filled the unemployment rolls, because Americans wouldn't harvest sugarcane.

When "Harvest of Shame" was filmed there was virtually no sugar grown in the region, known as the "Vegetable Capital of the World." But after Presidents Eisenhower and Kennedy boycotted Cuba's sugar, congressional subsidies turned the land into the largest mainland cane-growing region in the United States, and by 1975 Wedgworth Farms, the largest of the area's vegetable producers, which had been cited by Edward R. Murrow as an example of exploitation, went out of business because of the expanding sugar acreage.

Although cane was harvested mechanically in Louisiana, Texas, Hawaii, and Australia, in Florida it was cut by hand. The swampland did not hold the stalk straight, and machines had not been perfected to cut it efficiently. In 1974 farmworkers' minimum wage was $1.30 an hour, but canecutters earned $2.65 an hour. Even so, no farmworkers in Belle Glade or anywhere on the East Coast were willing to do the work, despite the growers' having fulfilled their legal requirement to conduct a search through the Labor Department's employment offices and to send round-trip bus tickets to interested applicants. Legal services attorneys had filed suit to stop growers from importing Jamaicans, arguing that the Jamaicans were taking work away from U.S. citizens. The court threw out the case because the attorneys could not find U.S. citizens willing to cut cane.

The work consisted of lifting a machete, or "cane knife," over one's head and striking the base of the plant next to one's foot. Although the sun was broiling and the heat and smoke from burning nearby cane fields added to the discomfort, the workers had to wear metal guards to protect their legs from being slashed by cane knives. Growers burned the fields before cutting them, so the thick black carbon from the sugar stalks covered the workers. Cutters worked a minimum of eight hours a day, and often for seven-day weeks. They frequently cut their legs and were occasionally bitten by one or another of the poisonous snakes in the Florida swamps.

It was not surprising that Americans were unwilling to do such work. Welfare, food stamps, moving to urban areas for even the lowest-paying and most degrading jobs, or waiting in early-morning lines for the dwindling field jobs were all preferable. On the other hand, in Jamaica unemployment was over 25 percent, there were no welfare or other social benefits, and sugarcutting jobs, which were hard to find, brought in as little as 15 cents an hour. Most of the migrant Jamaicans, who lived for more than six months in army-style barracks companies provided, had never cut cane before. Virtually all were married and had large families to support. In Jamaica cutting cane was considered slaves' work, and natives went to the other end of the island to do it because they would be disgraced to be known in their villages as canecutters. Even in this country they were so ashamed that they often left the stalks by the road uncut so they would not be seen. They needed so desperately to work that, when they could no longer handle the misery and loneliness of their jobs, there were reports that they would deliberately cut themselves with their cane knives, so they would be sent home without being blacklisted by the British West Indies Central Labour Organization, which recruited them on behalf of their government. If they were blacklisted, the reports said they would not be allowed back into the United States in the summer to earn as much as $75 a day in Virginia, West Virginia, New York, and Vermont picking apples, another job for which U.S. workers could not be found despite vigorous efforts to recruit and train them.

More than any other state, however, California demonstrated both the significance of alien farmworkers and how their presence affected other agricultural policy issues, particularly mechanization and immigration. Historically, growers had driven down wages and provided a supply of workers by importing workers not only from Mexico (people of Mexican origin made up the majority of the state's farmwork force), but also from the Philippines and, in the 1970s, from Arab countries and the Punjab section of India. Their legal status varied. They became citizens, were "resident legal aliens" with the same rights as citizens, had temporary visas such as the "green card," or were illegal. In 1976 the Immigration and Naturalization Service estimated there were as many as 6 million Mexicans living illegally in the United States.

In 1962, when Chavez first established his union, he needed the legal importation of Mexicans. As growers in the East legally imported Jamaicans to cut cane and pick apples, growers in California and throughout the Southwest imported thousands of Mexicans. When the season was over the Mexicans were shipped back home. The Mexican government liked the "bracero program" (from a Spanish word meaning "arm"), which alleviated that country's severe unemployment problem and injected the economy with wages earned abroad. The growers liked it because they got large numbers of workers who could be shipped home at the end of the season, and earlier if they caused trouble. For union organizers the braceros were a nightmare. Attempts to organize them failed. Growers used them to break strikes. Many organizers, who were of Mexican heritage, found it personally difficult to oppose giving jobs to Mexicans, especially since braceros often had friends and relatives in the United States. But they finally decided it was necessary. In 1964, after intense lobbying by Chavez and several labor unions, Secretary of Labor Willard Wirtz announced an end to the program.

But ending the program raised the number of illegal aliens crossing the border, and growers who had successfully broken strikes with braceros suddenly found themselves on the wrong side of the law when they tried to use "illegals." Chavez and his supporters turned in the "illegals" to the Border Patrol, then lobbied Congress to force the Immigration and Naturalization Service (INS) to conduct more raids and to deport Mexicans with less delay. The INS didn't change, but the lobbying intensified public sympathy toward the UFW. Growers argued that "illegals" were also members of Chavez's union, so what did it matter? But the issue was that growers were deliberately violating the law and being caught at it. The end of the bracero program gave Chavez the necessary breathing room to unionize. It also led growers, afraid of crops rotting in the field, to increase their mechanization dramatically — something Chavez strongly opposed. In 1963 most California tomatoes used by processors for ketchup, soups, and other canned or bottled products were harvested by hand. Machines harvested 1.5 percent of California's crop. By 1968 machines harvested 95 percent.

By the 1970s the unions discovered that they, too, had difficulty finding a stable labor force willing to do farm

work. In 1974 Chavez still talked about stricter border control and turning "illegals" over for deportation. Both the
UFW and the Teamsters recruited union workers in Mexico, maintained health clinics there for union members who
still lived there, and claimed that legal status was not their
concern. In 1976, when directors in local union offices of
both the UFW and the Teamsters along the border were
asked their position on illegal aliens, they regarded the question itself as hostile. As one director put it, "There are probably several right here in this room. We don't ask." Neither
the unions nor the growers cared whether workers were
citizens.

This acceptance of "illegals," which continues today, may
be only an interim period. The unionization in California
was the first success in the effort to turn agricultural work
into a well-paid and socially respectable trade, and similar
developments followed in Florida's orange groves and in
the rich Rio Grande Valley of Texas. Eventually, it may no
longer be necessary to go outside our borders to find farmworkers if wages rise high enough to be attractive to people
already here and rapid mechanization eliminates
backbreaking, dangerous occupations such as cutting cane
and lettuce by hand. Also, just as farmers in Iowa consider
farming worthy for their children, eventually farmworkers
in California may regard what they do as worthy for their
children.

Chavez taught that apparently cheap labor was actually
expensive because it was both inefficient and had high social
costs. He successfully showed that even the lowest-paid
farmworkers were valuable to our agricultural policy. More
significantly, the unionization of California's farmworkers
established a direction for agricultural labor nationwide,
just at a critical moment.

By 1976 it was clear that the farm population was rapidly
declining to a point below which it could not safely go. After
all, no matter how thoroughly an operation became

mechanized, someone had to decide what to plant, run the machine that planted it, watch over the crop while it was growing, harvest, and take the crop to market. Farming required farmers, who were disappearing.

California, with its high number of corporate farms staffed by agricultural wage-earners, was pointing the way for farmers nationwide. Traditionally family farmers could compete with larger, more heavily capitalized farms that had large payrolls because the family's labor helped absorb a loss for one season in the hope of profiting from the next. From 1967 to 1974, however, there was a consistent decline in the use of family labor. Farmers' children, who traditionally helped out when necessary, had migrated to the cities and suburbs for jobs. Even the housewife — a significant factor in the farm work force — was less available than in the past.

The individual farmer, even one who owned the land, was only a part of a larger factory-like process. Farmers might regard themselves as independent businesspeople producing chickens, hams, or corn under contract with large operations, but because of specialized production requirements and limited marketing options, the real difference between them and fulltime employees of a meat-packing plant was that their income was often more precarious.

As mechanization became more essential, farmers became more strongly locked into specializing in a particular crop that required a particular machine. The costs of machinery such as sixteen-row raddish-harvesters, combines that harvest, thresh, and bind twelve acres of wheat in an hour, and sugar-beet harvesters required large bank loans and large annual sales. The rising cost of land made it difficult for young farmers to own any acreage, but the high prices crops brought made it economical to develop a variety of leasing and other arrangements to work the land.

Meanwhile the commodity futures markets made it clear

that farmers needed to learn new skills. Producing large crops was no longer sufficient; one had to understand how to sell the crops by making what could often be complicated financial and marketing decisions.[2] Governmental subsidies no longer guaranteed a living wage, so a skilled farmer had to use a variety of technical, financial, and managerial techniques to keep costs low. Profits or losses no longer depended on simply owning the land or the machinery. Land owners began to realize that success required them to have an experienced farmer running the place. The farmer's skills were becoming valuable commodities in their own right.

Meanwhile food shortages were demonstrating to the public how it depended on the work of a small sector of the population. A shortage of sugar in 1974, for example, had resulted in hoarding and astronomical price increases.

If Chavez was successful in organizing the least trained of the country's farmworkers, then the farmers — the brains of the farm labor force — discovered they had considerable power over the country's food supply. During the 1970s they did little to actualize their power, although some made poorly organized attempts to do so. But the significance of their skills, as opposed to their capital, suddenly became manifest. For decades farmers' significance had been rhetorically appreciated, and few people had bothered to take the rhetoric to heart or to parse out why farmers were significant.

It was the curious combination of Earl Butz and Cesar Chavez who taught what long-term implications the changes in the agricultural labor force held for the country's food policy.

---

1. Much of this description of urban-based organizations devoted to migrants stems from the author's experience as an insider. In 1973 and 1974 he was editor of a newsletter for the Migrant Legal Action Program (MLAP) in Washington. MLAP's funds came from such various

government sources as the Office of Economic Opportunity, the Labor Department, and the Legal Services Corporation.

2. In 1984 farmers were buying computers and subscribing to agricultural data bases. Farmers purchased more personal computers per capita than most other occupations.

Chapter Nine

Good Harvests and the Terror They Bring

> If a psychoanalyst, testing his associations, had suddenly said to Mr. Salter the word "farm," the surprising response would have been "Bang!"—for he had once been blown up and buried while sheltering in a farm in Flanders. It was his single intimate association with the soil. It had left him with the obstinate though admittedly irrational belief that agriculture was something alien and highly dangerous.
>
> —*Scoop*
> by Evelyn Waugh

Under presidents Ford, Carter, and Reagan, the government became steadily more involved in subsidizing and controlling agriculture. This direction had little to do with ideology. Jimmy Carter, who campaigned to give farmers higher payments, unsuccessfully tried to limit them. Ronald Reagan, who campaigned for a market-oriented agriculture, created the largest and most expensive program in history for paying farmers not to produce.

The secretaries of agriculture who followed Butz found they were often powerless to make the government's agricultural decisions and were sometimes not even consulted when their presidents considered action. The chairs of the agriculture committees in Congress were too busy trying to get bills passed and signed to concern themselves with the overall objectives of agricultural policy. Presidents, secretaries of agriculture, and congressional leaders increasingly wondered aloud why the government had created expensive, inefficient programs that served no clear purpose.

During the more than four years that Earl Butz served as secretary, he frequently denounced as "instant experts" the consumer activists who complained about rising food prices. Nevertheless in 1975 he chose to fill the Agriculture Department's number-two spot with John A. Knebel, who seemed to fit Butz's own definition of an instant agriculture expert.

At his confirmation hearings, Knebel was asked his views of the tobacco program. He said, "Tobacco is to me a little cloudy. . . . And I must confess that I am just not current on it. I cannot tell you what my position is at this time." Senator Dick Clark voted against confirmation, noting that Knebel had never lived on a farm, had no agricultural education, and admittedly knew nothing about the subject until 1969, when he was hired as a lawyer by the House Agriculture Committee. But he was confirmed, and when Butz resigned as secretary of agriculture in October 1976, Knebel took his place.

When he resigned, Butz boasted of his accomplishments:

- Farmers no longer depended on government for their income.

- The government no longer bought and owned huge surpluses and no longer told farmers how much to plant.

- A market for agricultural exports was growing, bringing prosperity to farmers.

Ten days later Knebel, on President Ford's instructions, began undoing all these accomplishments. Knebel announced a 50 percent increase in the loan rate for wheat and a 20 percent increase for corn, even though the Agriculture Department had announced a month earlier that it would *not* raise loan rates. The increase was recommended by President Ford's political advisers, who believed giving payments to farmers right before the election could help Ford win. The farm vote was considered critical for a Republican president, and farmers were angry at Ford both because market prices were low and because Ford had imposed embargoes on selling grain abroad.

The USDA reversed its position so suddenly because Butz had been an unusually powerful secretary of agriculture and had restrained Ford when the president was tempted to give farmers payments. Ford, for example, had reluctantly vetoed legislation in 1975 raising target prices and loan rates for farmers, because if he didn't, Butz threatened to resign. In fact Butz's legislative success with the Agriculture and Consumers Protection Act of 1973 had severely limited the administration's power to give payments to farmers, and suddenly raising the loan rate was an unusual move that Butz opposed.

With Butz out of the way, Acting Secretary Knebel let the president and his top advisors make the decisions on agricultural policy, a practice the next two secretaries felt forced to accept. Knebel helped reinstitute large government-supported surpluses and payments to farmers. In 1975, for example, the government owned virtually no wheat; Knebel increased wheat under loan from 32 million bushels to 223 million bushels. By 1977 it was up to 740 million bushels, which the government was paying to store. In 1975 farm-income and price programs cost the government $800 million. In fiscal year 1977, which began in October 1976, these programs jumped to nearly $4.5 billion. A big part of the $4.5 billion was the cost of the pre-election loans.

On January 11, 1977, the Senate Agriculture Committee rapidly and unanimously approved forty-eight-year-old

Bob Bergland of Minnesota to be Jimmy Carter's secretary of agriculture. At first Congress was delighted with Bergland, who was the first farmer to become an agriculture secretary in twenty-two years. Bergland owned a 600-acre wheat farm (appraised at $440,000) near the Canadian border, was a graduate of the University of Minnesota's two-year School of Agriculture, and was also a four-term congressman serving as chair of an influential House Agriculture Committee subcommittee.

He was one of a small number of congressional farm leaders to whom representatives and even senators listened. He had a reputation for understanding the complicated details of farm legislation, for bringing coalitions together, and for eschewing publicity. At the confirmation hearings one senator noted, "He has the unique ability of not only winning the confidence of those of us from the farm states, the producer states; but he also won the respect of his colleagues from the big cities."

At first Bergland seemed well positioned to establish a good working relationship between the administration and Congress. President Carter promised to give his cabinet members autonomy to run their departments without White House interference and had selected Bergland at the recommendation of Vice President Mondale, one of the president's most influential advisors. Bergland was also recommended to Carter by Thomas Foley (a Democrat from Washington), chair of the House Agriculture Committee, one of the two most important farm-policy-makers in Congress. The other one was Herman Talmadge (a Democrat from Georgia), chair of the Senate Agriculture Committee, who told Bergland at the confirmation hearings, "We, of course, met many, many times on conference committees to adjust the differences between House-passed bills and Senate-passed bills. I have always been impressed with the way you have done your homework and the knowledge with which you spoke and commented in conference; and the thought that you did not deem it necessary to do all the talking in conference."

Butz's confirmation hearings had been long and often acrimonious, but the one-day Bergland hearings were filled with relaxed good humor and a feeling from both Republican and Democratic legislators that one of their own was finally going to be secretary. Republican Milton Young of North Dakota said, "I think you have the best background of any Secretary of Agriculture I have known for a long while. . . . As you know, I have got into kind of a bad habit in recent years of voting against the Secretaries of Agriculture. But I am going to change that and vote for you." Democratic Walter Huddleston of Kentucky quipped, "The only other question I have, Mr. Bergland, is how is your repertoire of ethnic jokes? We would like to keep you at least four years." Republican Robert Dole of Kansas, who ran against Carter as President Ford's running mate, said, "I certainly think that President-elect Carter has selected a well qualified and very capable man to be Secretary of Agriculture."

During the confirmation hearings the committee's primary interest was in a new farm bill. The expiring 1973 act had been created when market prices were high and governmental payments to farmers were not regarded as necessary. The act had established the concept of a target price; if market prices dropped below the target price, the government would pay the farmer the difference as a "deficiency payment." But target prices were well below market values and also below the farmer's production costs. In addition, each farmer could receive a maximum of only $20,000 in deficiency payments, too little to matter for most U.S. farmers, who had large operations.

The "loan rate" had become the figure most farmers looked to when considering the level of income protection available from the government. "Loan rate" was perhaps a misnomer, because if a farmer chose the option to default on the loan, which frequently happened when rates were high and market prices low, then the government simply took over ownership of the wheat. Butz had insisted that the target prices and, more important, the loan rates be below production costs so farmers would not be tempted to grow wheat for governmental payments and storage.

Even though the 1973 act had an escalator clause raising target prices and loan rates in subsequent years, the increases were insignificant compared to the rise in production costs. Butz had assumed that when prices were low in the free-market farm economy he helped create, that farmers would grow less. Instead in 1976 farmers planted a record 80 million acres of wheat, even though they had 1.1 billion bushels in storage and the U.S. market consumed less than 750 million bushels a year.

Meanwhile growth in the market was slowing. World grain surpluses were higher than they had been since 1971, and the good weather continued to reduce demand for U.S. exports. Senator Henry Bellmon (a Republican from Oklahoma) noted that it was even beoming difficult to give grain away under the Food for Peace program. "I recently had an opportunity to go to India and Bangladesh, and I was distraught to find that, for political reasons, our Government was about to unload a very large quantity of grain into these countries where they had an abundant crop this year. There is no need. They do not have storage even for what they grew. We are significantly destroying the market prices for the producers over there."

Perhaps farmers ignored the marketplace because they believed the government would help them out if they ran into financial trouble. After all, during the election Ford raised the loan rate, and Jimmy Carter told farmers, "We will make sure that our support prices are at least equal to the cost of production."

In 1977 farmers and the congressional agriculture committees were anxious to see whether Carter meant to keep his promise. The Senate committee was pleased that during Bergland's congressional service, he had regularly opposed Earl Butz, tried to protect farmers from free-market policies, and tried to save the Sugar Act. The committee expected Bergland, who said he supported higher target prices and loan rates, to fight for them within the Carter administration, especially during meetings with budget officials.

Bergland and the congressional farm leaders believed that a good bill required a careful balance. They liked the idea of a market-oriented agriculture, which had freed farmers from outmoded controls and given them record incomes. On the other hand, they believed it was necessary, at least in the short term, for the government to supplement farm income. "I favor the free market," Bergland explained, "but when I say free market, I don't mean bankrupt prices." The question was, how could government protect farmers from bankrupt prices without dominating agriculture?

Neither Bergland nor Congress wanted to return the USDA to controlling farmland or owning large surpluses, but if loan rates were raised too high, farmers would be encouraged to grow their crops for governmental storage again. The pre-election loans had already dramatically increased the amount of grain under loan, and Bergland wanted to avoid the USDA's taking ownership, or at least acquiring more. Acquiring and storing grain was expensive, and Carter had promised to balance the budget.

Bergland was also afraid high loan rates would discourage growth in export markets, which he considered essential for agricultural prosperity. He saw that high loan rates told the country's competitors the level at which to begin discounting their grain. Since the Australians, Canadians, Argentinians, and others were willing to undersell the United States, U.S. grain farmers would lose out in foreign markets. Both congressional leaders and Bergland agreed that the problem was how to increase target prices and loan rates enough to provide farmers necessary income without making them so high that the government would acquire huge surpluses, reduce competitiveness abroad, and destroy the free-market concept.

Nor was that the only balancing required. Although the primary objective was to raise grain farmers' income, the farm bill was comprehensive. It included payments for cotton, milk, wool, mohair, peanuts, soybeans, and sugar, and it renewed conservation, agricultural research, and rural development programs, thus enlisting the support of all farm legislators. It renewed the food-stamp and Food for Peace programs to get the critical support of representatives from urban and suburban areas.

Everyone understood that only a strong and respected secretary of agriculture had the trust and power necessary to lead a carefully balanced bill through Congress. Committee and subcommittee chairs were naturally interested in getting the best deal for their constitutents, but the most influential of them appeared willing to compromise their admittedly parochial interests if they believed following the secretary was in agriculture's best interest. These people trusted Bob Bergland, and they realized that if he was in charge of making agriculture policy for President Carter, he could use the considerable power of a threatened veto.

In agricultural legislation the presidential veto was especially powerful. Because the agricultural population had declined, fewer legislators were required by their constituents to care about farm policy. Putting together a coalition to pass bills by even a simple majority was becoming increasingly difficult and the votes to override a veto were not there. During consideration of the 1973 act a threatened veto shaped the debate by defining how far Congress could go. When President Ford vetoed the bill in 1975 because he thought it went too far, Congress could not find the necessary two-thirds to override. By 1977 it was common wisdom that the president's agreement was critical to turning a farm bill into law. Even without that power, Jimmy Carter was a Democratic president in the first year of his term, and the Democratic Congress was inclined to follow his lead.

Bergland knew when he was confirmed in January that he had little time to develop a legislative proposal. For the first time Congress was considering a major farm bill under its buget process. It had created the process to control its own spending, rather than depending on the executive branch for budget restraints and information. All committees were required to report significant spending bills to the full Senate and House by May 15 so Congress could know how much it was planning to spend during the year.

A major farm bill traditionally needed several months for hearings and redrafting before each agriculture committee finally voted. Bergland estimated that if the administration wanted to lead, it had to present a complete farm bill by the middle of March. First, however, the bill had to clear the president's own budget process.

On March 7 Bergland submitted the Agriculture Department's proposal to the president's Economic Policy Group (EPG). The EPG took longer than expected to make a decision, forcing Bergland to postpone his appearances before the congressional agriculture committees scheduled for March 14 and 15. On March 22, the day before Bergland's rescheduled Senate appearance, President Carter agreed with his budget people that Bergland's proposal was too expensive. According to J.B. Penn on the president's Council of Economic Advisors, Carter did not make the decision directly, but gave his budget people authority to overrule Bergland. They finally did so at the last minute. The secretary's prepared testimony had to be changed, and Bergland had little time to prepare a convincing defense for a proposal he didn't support.

For the next two days he told the Senate and House agriculture committees that the administration proposed a wheat target price of $2.60 for fiscal 1978 and a loan rate of $2.25. The committees believed that it cost more than $3.00 to produce a bushel of wheat, so these rates were disappointingly low. When asked what he really thought of the bill, Bergland said, "President Carter is committed to balancing the budget by 1981 and this is part of it." Bergland admitted that if he were a private citizen, he would have difficulty supporting the proposal he was making. Meanwhile someone in the administration had leaked the story to the newspapers that Bergland lost out in a private last minute confrontation with Charles Schultze, chair of the Council of Economic Advisors.

Bergland later summarized the absence of congressional support. "I didn't have any votes in the Senate Agriculture Committee," he explained, and of the forty-six members of the House Agriculture Committee, "I had five votes." Less than a month after the first proposal Carter agreed to higher support prices. The target price for wheat rose to $2.90 from $2.60.

In making the new proposal Bergland warned that it was Carter's highest offer, and if Congress passed a bill with farm payments costing more than $2.2 billion a year, it "faces a serious threat of veto." The Senate Agriculture Committee nevertheless passed a bill the administration said could cost up to $3.9 billion. In addition to raising wheat prices to $3.10 for fiscal 1978, the committee proposed giving farmers some immediate relief by raising the price 43 cents to $2.90 for fiscal 1977, which had begun in October 1976.

On May 23, before the full Senate voted on its committee's bill, Bergland announced Carter's third and final offer. The president would agree to a current increase of 18 cents if the Senate agreed to his lower rates for 1978 and beyond. He hoped the Senate would prefer giving farmers some money immediately rather than risk a veto.

But the Senate ignored the president, and in September Carter pointed out that he was signing the act reluctantly.

"I have to admit that the bill is about $300 million more costly than I had personally preferred to see." Although he was the first farmer to become president in this century, his only apparent interest in the farm bill was how it affected the total $66 billion deficit he had promised to end. Regarding that issue, Edmund Muskie (a Democrat from Maine), chair of the Senate Budget Committee and Carter's strongest supporter in Congress, complained because Carter did not follow through on his threat to veto. "The administration has capitulated to those advocating even higher farm income supports. . . . One wonders what further surprises are in store for those of us who believe that this administration is trying to control spending."

Carter made several major mistakes that contributed to the defeat. One was in allowing his Congressional liaison work to be handled ineptly. Four years later Ronald Reagan directly lobbied Congress, at one point even inviting key farm legislators to the Oval Office; but Carter let his spokespeople express his views, and the people representing him on the Hill were not always his best. For example several senators criticized the way the administration estimated the potential cost of the farm bill. Most of the criticism was self-serving or incorrect, but at a presentation before the Senate Agriculture Committee, administration budget analysts who didn't understand how the target price worked created unnecessary antagonism. They argued with senators who tried to correct them and continued to present their position based on their mistake. Weeks later senators were still angrily complaining about the incident on the Senate floor. Carl Curtis (a Republican from Nebraska) said, "I have heard nonsense before, but nothing like that I heard in the budget figures presented to the Committee on Agriculture, Nutrition, and Forestry. . . . Yet, they had the audacity to present that and say 'here is the danger to the budget.' It was not only nonsense; it was false."

Carter's biggest mistake on the farm bill, however, was

allowing his agriculture secretary's credibility to be undermined. Congress appeared willing to follow Bergland's lead.
If it were necessary for the secretary to present proposals
the agriculture committees didn't like, at least Bergland
could have done so as the president's chief agricultural
policy-maker. Instead he became a messenger, as the press
stories based on administration sources reported accurately.
Bergland had lost a critical fight on the most significant
piece of legislation during his tenure as secretary, and
during the next 4 years he never regained the lost stature.

The chairs of the Senate and House agriculture committees, both very capable and different people, assumed
responsibility for the 1977 farm bill. In 1971, when Herman
Talmadge became chair of the Senate's committee, he was
asked to comment on the seniority system. "The longer
I stay up here," he said, "the more I like it." As chair he
subjected the USDA to scrutiny it had not previously experienced. A former lobbyist pointed out his effectiveness:
"He doesn't make a lot of noise, but when he's done cir-
culating he's got a lot of votes."

By 1977 Talmadge had been elected four times and was
one of the most powerful members of Congress, more
powerful and influential than any subsequent chair of the
Senate Agriculture Committee is likely to be in the
foreseeable future. By 1979 his career was destroyed when
he was denounced by the Senate for "financial misconduct."
The reported financial shenanigans and his defense of them
made many people doubt his basic ability and made it difficult to appreciate just how effective he had been.

Certainly he was difficult to categorize. Even though his
famous populist father had been against New Deal farm
programs, calling them "downright Communism an' plain
damn-foolishness," Herman became one of their last significant congressional defenders. He considered himself the
champion of the little farmer, and his official biography once
began, "Of all his many accomplishments and distinctions,

Herman Talmadge prefers to be known as a farmer." He was a millionaire with one 1500-acre and another 2500-acre farm; the mansion on the second one became famous as Tara in *Gone With the Wind.* He had a ceramic cuspidor near his desk and was one of the Senate's last tobacco chewers, reportedly spitting in the Capitol's corridors where spittoons had once been.

Two weeks after the 1976 election, Talmadge held a party to introduce president-elect Carter to the most influential people on Capitol Hill. Talmadge had close ties to Majority Leader Robert Byrd, Finance Committee Chair Russell Long, and Armed Services Committee Chair John Stennis. He and Hubert Humphrey (a Democrat from Minnesota) were friends, and when Humphrey was discussed as a possible presidential candidate in 1971, Talmadge created a subcommittee on rural development and named Humphrey chair, a position that helped Humphrey attract publicity.

Talmadge paid attention to details often overlooked in the tedious legislative process. During a slow-moving markup session for a grain-inspection bill, Senator Humphrey had included a provision to inspect all interstate shipments. Talmadge opened his eyes and took the cigar out of his mouth. He observed that his constituents included poultry farmers along the border between Georgia and Florida who took their corn to a mill in Florida to be ground into chickenfeed. "If every time one of my constituents crosses the border for chickenfeed, he's got to get his corn inspected by some federal official who for all we know could be all the way up in Atlanta, then I'm going to be spending all my time on the phone talking to outraged chicken farmers. . . . " Humphrey instantly exempted small quantities of grain from inspection.

In 1977 Talmadge was ready to lead an omnibus farm bill through the Senate. He began preparing for the 1977 farm bill in June 1976. He explained that because of the congressional budget procedure, the "Committee will need to complete the process of public hearings earlier than in the past, to permit adequate time for drafting and markup of legislation before the [May 15] deadline." He asked current and former officials in the Agriculture Department, leaders of farm and consumer groups, academicians, and others to provide information and legislative suggestions. Their replies were published in September 1976 in the 277-page *Farm and Food Policy,* which included a history and description of the country's farm programs. As Talmadge explained in the introduction, the book helped focus "discussion and discourse necessary for Congress to prepare for its legislative responsibilities in the coming year."

On January 18, 1977, Talmadge was ready with a draft bill and told the Senate, "Any legislation of this . . . nature must be considered in the context of a total and comprehensive national food and agricultural policy. This is so because food is basic. . . . Our whole complex of agricultural law must have a basic purpose—the assurance to the consumers of this nation of a continuous supply of food and fiber at a reasonable price, and some assurance to the producers that they won't be bankrupted in that process." Named also for the committee's ranking Republican, Robert Dole, the Talmadge/Dole bill—in the absence of an acceptable bill from the administration—became the focus of debate not only in the Senate, but also in the House.

On February 22 Talmadge began seventeen days of hearings. More than 150 witnesses appeared, and the transcript ran more than 1800 pages. The House Agriculture Committee also held exhaustive hearings with a record of more than 1250 pages. Established farm groups testified, such as the American Farm Bureau Federation, the National Grange, and the National Farmers Organization. Established commodity groups testified, such as the National Cotton Council of America, the American Honey Producers Association, the Poultry and Egg Institute of America, the National Wood Growers Association, Riceland Foods, the

American Rice Growers Cooperative Association, the National Corn Growers Association, the National Association of Wheat Growers, and the American Soybean Association. Processors, manufacturers, bankers, environmentalists, nutritionists, consumer groups, business leaders, economists, ad hoc groups of farmers, individual farmers, and farmers' wives came to the hearings carrying their stacks of photocopied testimony. They wanted higher prices, lower prices, less governmental involvement, and more governmental involvement, and most gave their statements in empty rooms devoid of press attention where one token senator or congressman represented the committee.

Many witnesses believed that, unlike in 1973, there was talk of the government helping cover production costs, so perhaps if they asked for money, they might get it. This is what some of them told the House Agriculture Committee:

"I am Ernest Burkhart and I raise grain and livestock in south central Kansas located in Sumner County. . . . We are facing quite a grave financial situation. In my estimation it is going to be as bad as it was in the 1930s unless something is changed. . . . Farm management figures released in our area for 1976 show that the farmer that has been in business for many years had to spend $1.12 to produce each $1.00 of income. The young farmer who is trying to buy land and put together a line of machinery to farm with was forced to spend $1.50 for each $1.00 of income in 1976. Two years ago these same farmers were spending 60 cents to 70 cents for each dollar of income. We cannot continue to spend more than we make each year. . . . Therefore, we need relief now."

Earl L. Strong, the president of the Nebraska Grain Producers Association said, "I am a corn and soybean grower. We're not complaining too much right now, but it's what we see in the future. . . . [W]e see a build up of one billion bushel carryover of wheat and enough extra corn production to hold down the price of wheat below the cost of production and the price of corn enough to take most of the profit out of raising corn. . . . We recommend that the price support loans be 100 percent of the cost of production."

"I am Karen Smith, a farm wife and mother of three, from Burlington, Colo. I don't claim to be a polished speaker, especially when I'm away from my own stomping grounds. Several months ago, however, I decided I'd seen enough unfair injustices heaped upon farmers' shoulders. I decided I could no longer sit back and do nothing as the efforts of my husband and men like him were taken for granted by a nation of people with full bellies and cheap grocery bills."

"I am L. C. 'Clell' Carpenter, Vice President of Mid-continent Farmers Association, headquartered in Columbia, Missouri. . . . The sharp inflation in land values in just the last few years was unprecedented. But, these higher values are now built-in costs which must be recovered if farmers are to continue to produce at a profit. This is the price society must pay for the lack of an effective farm program in recent times when shortfalls in production and depleted reserves caused sharp, short-term increases in farm commodity prices, which in turn raised producers' expectations for the future and reflected this hope in spiraling land prices."

These hearings were important to both Talmadge and Foley. For agriculture committee chairs, power consisted of being able to give out money. Since they had money to give out in 1977, the least they could do was give the agricultural interests they regarded as their constituents an opportunity to ask for it. Many witnesses were likely to get something, and perhaps they might attribute their governmental payments to the personal intervention of the chairs.

The hearings also helped them keep in touch. Talmadge and Foley knew, after years of hearing and reading testimony, that witnesses tend to overstate their cases.

Farmers and their organizations seemed especially prone to hyperbole, perhaps because so few people paid any attention to what they said. During the boom years of the mid-1970s, when net income was skyrocketing, farmers complained that each year was the worst since the Great Depression. Talmadge and Foley had become adept at understanding the nuances and knowing when the distress was rhetorical and when it was real. They were worried because net income was down, farmers' debt was high, and without governmental action there seemed no way to prevent low prices from going lower.

On April 19 Talmadge was ready to mark up a bill, the final stage of the committee process. The bill was read aloud word by word, giving committee members an opportunity to understand, rewrite, and vote on the final language. Traditionally Congress held these often informal meetings behind closed doors, because they were where deals were struck, members revealed their ignorance of bills authored in their names, and the staff took a direct role in redrafting legislation. As part of the post-Watergate reform, however, meetings were opened to the public. Thus Talmadge's markup sessions were open.

Talmadge was probably the Senate's earliest riser and got up between three and four every morning. He insisted that the sessions begin at the unusually early hour of eight. The meetings were too important to miss, so for twelve consecutive mornings, including weekends, most of the committee's eighteen senators were there. They joked, because one didn't actually complain to a powerful Senate chair, that they were emulating the rising habits of farmers.

The senators worked from a specially printed copy of the Talmadge/Dole bill, which also contained a copy of the administration's bill for comparison. Most staff members had a specialty, and as each provision of the bill was discussed, the subcommittee staff specialist explained provisions and answered questions. Staff from the budget offices of Congress and the Agriculture Department, assistant secretaries of agriculture, and lobbyists from farm, commodity, and other interest groups answered questions. The formal meetings lasted about two hours, and the staff then rewrote sections the senators had voted to change. Sometimes lobbyists were successful in restoring language that had been changed, requiring a new vote the following morning.

This slow process was where major policy decisions were made and skillfully expressed after the staff spent hours carefully considering complicated statistical formulas.

The bill said, for example, "Loans . . . on each crop of wheat shall . . . be made available at . . . not less than 85 percent of the cost of production." But what did "cost of production" mean? The cost of producing wheat in Kentucky was higher than in Kansas. Should the cost include land costs? A farmer who inherited land paid lower production costs than one who had just bought. Wouldn't Congress reward the real-estate speculators who had caused land costs to skyrocket if it used the current high cost of land as the basis for subsidizing farmers? These issues were decided by defining "cost of production" to include land and to use nationally averaged costs.

By the time the committee reported the bill out by a vote of 18–0, the loan rates gave all wheat farmers 85 percent of production costs. This assured a profit to efficient farmers in better growing areas who had owned their land for several years.

Talmadge introduced his bill to the Senate on May 23 and began two days of lackluster debate in which he was firmly in control. Much of the time only three or four senators were present. Twenty-one amendments, mostly making minor changes and requiring the agriculture chair's support, were adopted by voice vote. The Senate repeatedly stopped to summon senators so they could introduce the amendments they had authored or to vote when parliamentary rules required an eleven-vote minimum.

At one point Carl Curtis complained, "A while ago I saw in the Chamber another Senator who was not on the Agriculture Committee. I was hoping he was going to stay. I wanted to convince him." Jesse Helms (a Republican from North Carolina) agreed: "As the Senator from Nebraska has indicated . . . the only Senators present are the members of the Agriculture Committee. We have discussed and debated this subject up and down. . . . Senators will then come in. They will ask somebody, 'How shall I vote?' Senators will cast their votes without hearing a syllable of debate. That will be it. It seems a very poor way to operate the world's greatest deliberative body."

Except for John Heinz (a Republican from Pennsylvania), who was ignored, no senator questioned whether it was wise to create major multi-year governmental programs to provide farmers with income. Heinz said, "The American farmer deserves better than having the Government interfere in his life. The Government is big enough and our farmers do not want a welfare program like this one. As it is, I would not advocate leaving the farmer entirely to the fates of the free market, but neither will I swing to the other extreme and advocate a system of agricultural socialism, and that is what this bill proposes."

The only significant debate on the bill concerned its cost, the sole reason President Carter gave for threatening a veto. But Carter had repeatedly changed his requirements for an acceptable bill. As a result the administration admitted that the difference between the president's and the Senate's bill was relatively insignificant. Howard W. Hjort, the Agriculture Department's chief economist, whom the *National Journal* called "the Administration's intellectual point man," later admitted, "the budget question has been blown out of proportion." The veto threat had evolved into Carter trying to establish that he, not Congress, was in control. Senator Dole and others noted that Carter would have difficulty justifying a veto after campaigning for support prices that equaled production costs.

Several senators tried to defuse the cost issue by arguing the budget estimates were unfair, since the Agriculture Committee could not use its own figures and had to accept the administration's and the Congressional Budget Office's estimates. These estimates were too high, committee members argued. They said if more realistic estimates were used, the opposition to their bill would disappear.

Hubert Humphrey said, "My colleagues . . . have not been able to convince those in the Department of Agriculture and the Office of Management and Budget. I hope the OMB will review my remarks and, if they think I have been unfair, come to my office and we will see just how unfair I can be. . . . I think I know a little bit more about agriculture than some of those people down there with their computers taking a look at what they call the outlays."

The senators discussed assumptions about the weather and the loan rate. If the weather continued to be good for several years, crops would be large, lowering prices and costing the government more money. But if the weather were bad, crops would be destroyed, raising prices and reducing costs.

"To me it seems absolutely ridiculous to assume 'abnormally good weather,'" Senator Dole said, "over the next 5 years as the administration does. . . . I am surprised at Secretary Bergland for embracing such a concept. After becoming secretary he attacked the previous administration for basing crop production estimates on 'normal' weather by citing his own experiences as a farmer who had experienced 'normal weather' twice in 27 years. Now he is attempting to beat down reasonable price support levels for farmers by application of cost estimates that will never materialize unless we have 'abnormally good' weather for 5 years in a row."

Concerning the loan rate, senators argued that the bill was a temporary expedient to deal with the short-term problem of low market prices. After all, they said, world population was still growing. Bad weather and other events could suddenly reduce current surpluses, causing prices to go up. If prices went up, then farmers who had taken out loans on their wheat, corn, and other commodities would reimburse the government. Furthermore the cost of providing adequate income "insurance" to farmers would be negligible.

The budget estimators assumed correctly, however, that prices would not go up high enough for farmers to repay the loans, and the government would also be paying large storage costs. Senator Humphrey said, "The budgeting process on price support loans for agriculture is an outrage, to put it as simply and as timidly as I can. It is as if the loans were made with no collateral. The Commodity Credit Corporation makes these loans and receives the best collateral in the world; namely, the product of the farm. Yet our budget process presumes that every dollar that is loaned is an expense and most likely will never be repaid."

The cost issue that most significantly affected the Senate debate was raised not by the administration, but by Edmund Muskie, chairman of the Budget Committee; he argued that the farm bill violated the Senate's own budget process. Eleven days earlier the Senate agreed to its First Concurrent Resolution, putting a cap on all spending for the year by the Agriculture Committee and others. The resolution included the cost of the farm bill. Afterward the Agriculture Committee immediately decided to give wheat farmers higher target prices. These deficiency payments for fiscal 1977, Muskie estimated, exceeded the budget resolution by $500 million.

Muskie argued that if the committee wanted to give farmers the money, it should have decided before the budget resolution. Instead the farm bill flagrantly violated the budget resolution passed only eleven days earlier. If the bill passed, he said, the Senate would be showing it didn't believe in the budget process. Therefore he introduced an amendment to delete the $500 million.

Pete Domenici (a Republican from New Mexico) said that the situation currently facing wheat farmers was a disaster, much like a flood, requiring extraordinary action. "We do not plan for disasters in that First Concurrent Resolution . . . and . . . there is not a Senator around that is unwilling to break it for a disaster. I say to my friends in the Senate that the wheat farmers in America are in a disaster, just as surely as the disaster that came when the Teton burst."

Carl Curtis, whose argument has been repeated in recent years, reasoned that Congress spent miniscule amounts on farm programs compared to food stamps. "Here we have a situation with desperately low wheat prices for the first time in many years. . . . Here is a farm bill, and the welfare part of it is about three times the cost of the agriculture part. . . .

"The food stamp program was started in 1964. It only cost $360 million. This year it is going to reach nearly $6 billion. . . . We . . . will increase this . . . by somewhere between $2 and $2.5 billion.

"I ask the distinguished chairman of the Budget Committee, if we adopt his amendment regarding wheat, how much will it lessen the Federal deficit? By $500 million. . . . Mr. President, the national debt cannot be paid with resolutions; the budget cannot be balanced with resolutions. You have to lower expectations, and if in the name of economy you want to lower expenditures, turn to the big items of the bill."

Muskie angrily told his colleagues, "Well, it is too bad, gentlemen. It is just too bad. But I am not going to walk away from this floor and fail in my duty to the Senate. This bill busts the budget."

Heinz supported Muskie: "It used to be that when a committee reported a measure to the full Senate, it was presumed worthy and usually routinely approved. The Federal cash register kept clinging and clanging from all those sales that were run up. . . . [T]his is precisely why Congress finally got around to establishing a budget committee that would have the responsibility to step back a little ways and take a good and hard look at overall spending, to weigh priorities, and to set reasonable limits."

Muskie lost by a vote of 50–46. The Senate then went on to pass the Talmadge/Dole bill easily sixty-nine to eighteen, without making substantial changes.

The bill's supporters saw its need from various perspectives, as some of them told the Senate:

George McGovern (a Democrat from South Dakota) said, "We are going to be voting a little later this year on a minimum wage proposal that again is designed to try to insure that the workers in this country at least have enough to meet the reasonable standards of life. I do not see how we can do any less for the wheat farmers of the country."

Another senator said that the bill had the advantage of being farsighted because farmers were not currently in a crisis, and this helped prevent one.

Henry Bellmon said, "While this legislation deals with farmers, it also has great impact on the conditions in our cities. The problems we have in our cities in so many cases have their genesis in the fact that rural economics have been so bad in the past that a lot of people have been forced out of agriculture and into the cities, where a lot of them are now living in poverty with great hardships, causing serious problems for the urban centers."

Strom Thurmond (a Republican from South Carolina) said, "Properly implemented, it will combine the best points of a market-oriented agriculture with reasonable guarantees of market stability, achieved by spreading the costs of agricultural risk among all of us who depend on farm products for survival." Thurmond complimented the Agriculture Committee on producing a careful balance so that government payments would be high enough to protect farmers "against sudden, drastic declines in commodity prices" but "below average total costs of production" to let "market demand" work and "to avoid excessive payments and unwanted surpluses."

Milton Young said, "With agriculture as the single most important segment of our entire economy, the Federal Government will have to do much more than they are thinking about now if they are to avert another economic disaster not unlike the 1930's . . . [T]arget prices in this bill . . . are already too low, . . . lower than almost every farm organization and almost every farmer believes they should be."

Dick Clark (a Democrat from Iowa) said, "I believe this is a fair and workable support system, and that these levels are adequate. They will cover most costs of production for most farmers, but will not guarantee farmers a profit. They should give farmers the support they need, but not so high as to price us out of world markets or attract land speculators to come into agriculture and bid land prices out of reach of farmers."

Meanwhile Thomas Foley was having trouble leading the bill through the House of Representatives. Foley, a forty-eight-year-old lawyer from Spokane, represented the state of Washington's Fifth Congressional District — the eastern part of the state. It was a sparsely populated expanse of some of the richest farmland in the country; the topsoil in some areas was believed to be 200 feet deep. Most of the district's voters were prosperous, white, and conservative. Throughout the 1970s Foley, the fastest-rising liberal in the House's leadership, barely won his elections back home.

His constituents did not feel entirely comfortable with a representative who got high voting ratings from the Americans for Democratic Action, the American Civil Liberties Union, and the AFL–CIO's Committee on Political Education. In addition, his primarily Republican constituents neither cared for his role as a leader of congressional Democrats nor his support of President Carter.

On the other hand, being chair of the House Agriculture Committee was a definite asset, because he could help provide farm payments to constituents. Payments first had to be enacted into law, however, so Foley needed to get an acceptable bill through his own committee.

But he had problems controlling his committee, which he had chaired for only two years. He had become chair when the most reform-minded Congress in recent history, elected in the aftermath of the Watergate scandal, met in Democratic Caucus to reorganize itself. One powerful committee chair resigned, and three were unseated. The ninety-two new representatives, in a startling display of freshmen's power, elected Foley chair of the Agriculture Committee even though he had voted against himself.

The move not only surprised Foley, it put him in an awkward position. He had served in Congress for only ten years, a remarkably short period to become a chair. His unseated predecessor, W.R. (Bob) Poage (a Democrat from Texas), had been in Congress since 1937 and was still a member of the committee. Poage had served in the House with Lyndon Johnson and still held the loyalty of the old-guard farm Democrats, who respected his detailed knowledge of agricultural policy, believed in the autocratic way he had ruled, and were suspicious of Foley, who had been head of the liberal Democratic Study Group and owed his position as chair to the reformers.

The Agriculture Committee that year, 1975, had more than twenty freshmen members. In contrast to previous years, a position on the committee was not only desirable, it was the most requested assignment because of rising food prices and the headlines they generated. The new members had already rebelled at strong seniority-based committee rule, and Foley had to convince these young Turks that it was in their own long-term interest to vote for measures they did not necessarily believe in.

If Foley could not get bills through his own committee, his effectiveness as a congressional leader would decline. It would also decline if he couldn't get the House to approve the bills he reported, as Poage discovered when he unexpectedly lost key votes on the House floor during the tumultuous Butz years. The 1977 farm legislation was Foley's first big test.

Foley did not have a prepared bill ready when he called for hearings. Although the witnesses sounded the same as they had before the Senate committee, in theory the Senate hearings had received comment on the Talmadge/Dole bill, and the House was hearing recommendations for what to provide in a bill.

When the House concluded its hearings after sixteen days, Foley asked his subcommittees to write the sections of a farm bill that related to their specialties. The resulting bill would have cost $6.2 billion a year in income support for farmers, compared to the projected $3.9 billion in the Senate's bill and $2.2 billion in the administration's bill. Foley said, "It won't help farmers for us to pass a bill the President won't sign." The committee let Foley and Poage develop a compromise that would also be acceptable to the administration, and Foley returned with a $2.3-billion bill that reduced the target price for wheat for 1978 from $3.20 to $3.00.

The committee debated the price angrily. By a vote of 23–22, Foley won what Keith Sebelius (a Republican from Kansas) called a "last minute showdown." Sebelius and

Foley both voted proxies on behalf of absent members. Foley said that farmers "can't eat" committee votes that are "absolutely meaningless unless they're enacted into law." Some Republican members reportedly voted for high price supports because they were against any legislation at all and hoped that the expensive bill would pass and be vetoed. There were also reports that Foley compromised over food stamps to attract the critical one vote.

Defending the winners' perspective, Richard Nolan (a Democrat from Minnesota) said, "Wheat farmers, who need help the most desperately, have been abandoned by the Carter administration." But in a written dissent, Paul Findley and Edward R. Madigan (both Republicans from Illinois) argued, "The committee recommendations . . . will have the effect of aggravating the already trouble-prone wheat sector by stimulating overproduction at a time of surplus and depressed prices."

The committee reported the bill out on May 16, but the House did not get around to debating it until July, when large grain crops were already coming to market and lowering wheat prices to less than $2 a bushel in some places. Meanwhile representatives from wheat-growing areas were lobbying intensely to raise target prices in 1977 to $2.90, the same current-year increase that the Senate passed and President Carter said he would veto. Many wheat farmers came to Washington to lobby Congress and the USDA. Secretary Bergland, rather than reiterating the administration's established position, told a group of wheat-block congressmen that the "equity is with you."

Glenn English (a Democrat from Oklahoma) and Keith Sebelius led the effort to raise the price, encouraged because Sebelius had lost in committee by only one vote. English explained to the *Congressional Quarterly,* "The chances of passing [the amendment on the floor] appeared unlikely, with a 9–1 urban majority and with the administration and the leadership against us." But the ad hoc congressional wheat block was willing to do a lot of vote-trading. House Budget Committee Chair Robert Giaimo (a Democrat from Connecticut) later complained, "Members from urban areas have accepted, without protest, this massive increase in commmodity supports. . . . This quid pro quo appears to be the support of farm-state members for the food stamp program and a higher minimum wage."

The Consumer Federation of America, which generally opposed farm payments, supported English and Sebelius's effort as "a symbolic effort on our part to strengthen the consumer-farmer alliance" and denied that in return the wheat block would vote for a consumer-protection agency.

In more than eight days of debate the House considered about seventy amendments; one representative wondered whether the bill had ever been to committee. Several members charged that vote trade-offs had been made. As part of a measure to lift planting restrictions, the price of peanuts was raised to a level one representative claimed was nearly 50 percent higher than the cost of production. Andrew Maguire (a Democrat from New Jersey) complained, "Some members . . . have said that they were going to get what they were going to get for the crops that were grown in their areas if they went along with the peanut subsidy. . . . I think we ought to end the process of that kind of log-rolling in this House."

The representatives created a new program that provided subsidies for sugar and gave the USDA the authority to acquire surpluses to keep the price high. Paul Findley observed, "I have always been impressed, and never more so than today, with the effectiveness of the sugar interests in this country, even though sugar is grown in relatively few congressional districts. Sugar interests certainly can find the right nerve centers in every congressional district of the country."

Later when Republican James (Jim) Johnson from a sugar-producing district in Colorado seemed to renege on a reported deal not to oppose the tobacco program, William Natcher (a Democrat from Kentucky) said, "I recall distinctly that last week, when sugar was in trouble . . . about 20 states which produce tobacco marched right down the road with that gentleman. They do not produce any sugar . . . in Kentucky. But when sugar is in trouble, sugar beets and sugar cane, the people in Kentucky are concerned about it." Earlier Robert E. Bauman (a Republican from Maryland) complained that it was "the height of cynicism to marry the food stamp program to the agriculture bill." He called it "political logrolling to gain votes for both."

The political logrolling had worked because by the time the House met to consider the farm bill, there were enough votes to pass the English-Sebelius amendment. In a surprise move Foley, rather than opposing the increases, offered them himself. He said, "The cost . . . is not insignificant, but the need is not insignificant either." He preferred offering an amendment he opposed to losing a significant fight. He was especially concerned that if higher target prices for wheat passed in spite of Democratic opposition, Republican representatives could take credit for the victory and say the Democrats had gone back on their promise to help farmers cover production costs.

Foley used the awkward situation to his advantage. Before the vote he got President Carter to agree not to veto a bill because of the 1977 price increases. In return he promised to support an amendment giving the secretary of agriculture authority to take cropland out of production as a condition for government payments. *The Wall Street Journal* later called the agreement " . . . the most important deal in the farm bill's evolution." On the floor Foley raised 1977 wheat prices to $2.90, avoiding additional increases for subsequent years.

Budget chair Giaimo told his colleagues, "I believe the House has gone too far." Findley said, "Note these facts. . . . This bill will guarantee profit on unlimited production of dairy products. It will do the same for wheat . . . for rice . . . for corn. Government guaranteeing profit means that we are going to get a tremendous production of these commodities, not in response to the marketplace, to consumer needs, to user prospects, but in response to Government enticement. And, of course, this will mean enormous pressure downward on prices in the long term, creating high Government payments, enormous payments that will be far higher than even Mr. Giaimo estimated."

The House was not convinced. The farm bill easily passed by a vote of 294 to 114.

When delegates of the House and Senate met in conference on August 1 to work out the more than 500 differences between their two versions of the farm bill, they were rushed. They wanted to finish so Congress could approve a final bill before adjourning in five days. The farm community would be anxious if it had to wait until September, when Congress was scheduled to return. Farmers and their bankers wanted to know how much government would provide before they planted their 1978 crops. For some it was already too late.

The major differences concerned a new sugar program and price supports for grain. Bergland wrote the conferees that it was "absolutely essential" to drop the sugar program, which had been added to the House bill and would increase food costs by up to $1 billion. Instead the conferees lowered support prices.

Although Bergland paid an unusual personal visit to the conference committee to help resolve the differences over grain supports, he was ineffective. Humphrey persuaded the Senate to use the House's lower figure to determine increased production costs, which were used to calculate increases in target prices and loan rates after 1978. In a dramatic last-minute move an observer handed Humphrey a slip of paper suggesting a formula for determining the 1978 wheat target price. The House bill provided for $3 a bushel, the Senate $3.10. The conferees agreed to Humphrey's formula of $3.05 if the 1978 wheat crop were less than 1.8 billion bushels, and $3 if the crop were larger. They hoped this formula would encourage farmers to grow less and would encourage the secretary of agriculture to invoke a provision in the new law giving him power to take land out of production.

They reached the last major agreement on the last day of the congressional session. But although they had held round-the-clock meetings for five days, they did not meet their deadline. After the recess the Senate approved the final bill by a vote of 63–8 on September 9. The House approved it 283–107 on September 16. When the president signed it on September 29 he said, "I think the cost of this bill, because of its wise drafting, will be less and less as the future years go by."

The cost did not go down. The 1977 act raised target prices, increased the maximum individual payments to $50,000, and raised the loan rates. For fiscal 1977 the target price for wheat was $2.90 and the loan rate $2.25. The first full year covered by the four-year bill was 1978, when the wheat target price increased to $3.05.

Farmers did not receive $3.05, however. Instead President Carter, whose original proposal for 1978 had been $2.25, signed a new bill in 1978 raising that year's price to $3.40 and providing for still higher supports in future years. He did so even though net farm income had increased that year by 29 percent.

In 1979 Carter agreed to a House plan to raise 1980's price even higher to $3.63; the 1977 act would have provided $3.06. By 1981, the last year of the four-year act, Carter had allowed the target price for wheat to rise to $3.81 and the loan rate to $3.20.

Early in his term Carter ended all pretense that the government was subsidizing farmers only temporarily and was not interfering with market-oriented agriculture. Farmers' income had become dependent on governmental payments, which were often above production costs and encouraged them to grow more. As a result Carter instituted expensive but unsuccessful programs to pay farmers to grow less.

The 1977 act had also authorized the secretary of agriculture to withhold land from production; unlike the New Deal legislation Butz had dismantled, however, the law didn't give the secretary the power to compel farmers not to grow. Although some farm-block representatives might have preferred them, mandatory land controls were regarded as too unpopular, especially since the administration and Congress were still rhetorically committed to market-oriented agriculture. Instead the secretary had the authority to ask for "voluntary" set-asides. Farmers could ignore the requests, but if they did, they became ineligible for deficiency payments and loans.

On August 29, 1977, when Bergland was on vacation, Deputy Secretary of Agriculture John White asked wheat farmers to take 20 percent of their cropland out of production. White explained that authority for the set-aside was provided in the 1977 farm bill, which would soon be passed by Congress, and Humphrey's conference compromise had encouraged the secretary to implement the provision. White had emphasized, "We are not paying people not to plant." Later that year the USDA announced a 10 percent set-aside for corn and a 10 percent "diversion" program in which the agency paid farmers 20 cents for each bushel of corn they did not plant.

In 1978 the USDA announced it would repeat the program. Even though farmers took 13 million acres of cropland out of production, however, they produced 300 million bushels more wheat than the year before. To keep grain surpluses from lowering market prices, the Carter administration expanded its programs for acquiring grain.

The 1977 farm bill had given the secretary authority to acquire up to 700 million bushels of wheat; but to avoid making it look as though the government once again owned huge surpluses, Congress said the farmers legally owned the grain, and it established long-term interest-free loans with the USDA paying farmers to build bins and store the grain. Bergland called his rapidly expanding storage programs "farmer-owned reserves." By January 1980 the country's bins were filled with 1.7 billion bushels of wheat, and by the end of the year an additional 2.4 billion bushels had been harvested.

The primary reason that the farm economy had not already collapsed under the glut was that export markets were still growing. On January 4, 1980, however, President Carter announced that because the Soviets had invaded Afghanistan, he was embargoing grain sales to the Soviet Union even though he knew from the 1976 campaign that the farm community was outraged by presidential grain embargoes.

At the 1976 Republican convention Gerald Ford pledged, "We will never use the bounty of America's farmers as a pawn in international diplomacy. There will be no embargoes." But Ford had imposed three grain embargoes in less than two years. He had tried to defuse this issue by running with Senator Robert Dole of Kansas, who had said earlier that year, "I am not certain President Ford will ever recover from that [the embargoes] in rural America."

In August 1976 Jimmy Carter had told an audience at the Iowa State Fair, "I understand the Republicans have just decided they don't like the idea of peanut farmers leaving their crops to look for new jobs in Washington. They've even agreed to stop the embargoes for a while to make farming more attractive so I'll stay in Plains. But I prefer to go on from my farm to the White House and stop embargoes once and for all!"

Less than an hour later Carter told a newspaper's interviewer, "Anyone in his right mind would not rob our people of food and create hunger in this country to sell food overseas." The *Des Moines Register* ran the headline, "Carter Leaves Door Open to Future Grain Embargoes After Saying He Wouldn't Impose Them — Conflicting Stands During Interview, State Fair Speech."

The next day Bob Dole waved the newspaper and told the Iowa State Fair, "Yesterday's speaker told you that he would end embargoes 'once and for all'. . . . And just an hour after his pledge to this state fair audience he apparently had a change of heart. He told interviewers that his language had been too strong, that he really would leave the door open to future grain embargoes. So, what appeared at 9:30 yesterday morning to be an unequivocal position is now burdened with a loophole. Which position on grain embargoes does he support this afternoon? I don't know and you don't know either."

Asked by reporters to explain Carter's position, Press Secretary Jody Powell said that Carter opposed a grain embargo but might be forced to impose one in the unlikely event that the U.S. food supply were in danger.

Less than four years later President Carter imposed a grain embargo even though no domestic food shortage existed. In *Keeping Faith, Memoirs of a President,* Carter explained, "The day after the take-over of Afghanistan, I decided not to go to Iowa. . . . My next decision would have an even more significant impact on the people of Iowa — whether or not to impose a grain embargo on the Soviet Union. Other economic steps would have some effect, but an analysis of possible sanctions revealed that this was the only one which would significantly affect the Soviet economy. . . . Such a step would be drastic, and especially difficult for me. During the early 1970s, President Nixon had repeatedly imposed grain embargoes in an attempt to stabilize domestic market prices, and in the 1976 campaign I had promised not to do so unless our nation's security was at stake. I knew that some farmers had interpreted my statements as a pledge not to interfere with the free marketing of grain under any circumstance."

Carter apparently did not even consult with his secretary of agriculture before taking the most significant agricultural policy action of his administration and the only one he mentioned in his memoirs. If he had talked to Bergland, the secretary might have informed him about recent embargoes. Nixon hadn't "repeatedly imposed grain embargoes"; he had imposed only one, the soybean embargo of 1973. Both presidents Nixon and Ford found that embargoes were not effective because, among other reasons, the secrecy and autonomy of the grain trade made it almost impossible to know how much was being purchased, let alone prevent grain from reaching its buyer. Even if Carter had been able to foretell its consequences, he still might have imposed the embargo. But in his memoirs, he called the embargo "very effective" and believed that its impact on the farm community was minimal because "we were to be successful, breaking the all-time world record in grain sales during 1980, in spite of the restraints on Soviet trade."

Later Bergland told NBC television that secrecy in the grain trade had made it impossible to know how much the Soviets had purchased and received. Nor did the embargo affect all shipments under the expiring U.S.-Soviet grain agreement, but only the ones over the limit of 8 million metric tons. Also, because foreign purchases were made in advance, the embargo affected trade not in 1980, but in subsequent years.

Even before the embargo many experts worried that high governmental supports were causing the United States to lose its share of growing foreign markets. The Argentinians, Brazilians, Canadians, Australians, and other competitors had benefited from the disruptions the previous embargoes caused. They expanded their acreage because foreign buyers believed they were more reliable. The embargo in 1980 let competitors expand their acreage still further, and in 1982, for the first time in a decade, U.S. agricultural exports actually declined. They fell $3 billion from the previous year and continued to decline in 1983.

Over a ten-year period the United States had slipped from being grain customers' first market to being their last. Because this country was no longer the preferred supplier, and the world was glutted with excess grain, some experts were beginning to question whether U.S. agriculture might be better off if it stopped producing for the export market. By the early 1980s the country was both selling its grain in world markets for less than production costs and also subsidizing the sales with tax dollars. By 1981, when President Reagan lifted Carter's embargo—in the midst of boycotting pipeline supplies to the Soviet Union—it was too late to repair the damage.

The Senate unanimously confirmed John Block, Ronald Reagan's secretary of agriculture, on January 22, 1981. The forty-six-year-old Block had graduated from West Point. After three years of active duty as an infantry officer, he returned to his boyhood home, his father's 300-acre, 200 hogs-per-year farm in Knox County, Illinois, and dramatically expanded it. At his confirmation hearings Block told the Senate Agriculture Committee that mortgages on his land ranged between $3 million and $5 million, and operating loans ran up to $200,000. Not including the salary he paid himself, his annual share of the farm's profits was $63,796. Representative Paul Findley told the committee, "He is a successful farmer. He has operated a family farm, but to give us an idea of how family farms have changed, it is now a 3,000 acre operation producing . . . around 6,000 heads of hogs every year. That is a lot of corn, . . . hogs, . . . land, . . . management, and it remains a family operation. . . . [I]t speaks well for John Block that he has been able to put together a farming unit of that size, keep it as a family unit and make it profitable."

At the confirmation hearings several senators wanted Block to assure them he would primarily represent the interests of farmers like himself. Secretary Bergland had angered producers by appointing people called consumer "activists" during the campaign and by objecting to using federal research funds to mechanize the fruit and vegetable industries still more. Bergland's assistant secretary, Carol Tucker Foreman, who had formerly been head of the Consumer Federation of America, had introduced initiatives to stop the use of sodium nitrite, a meat preservative Block believed was safe; to prohibit adding pulverized meat bones to hamburger and other products; and to provide consumers with more extensive food-grading and -labeling information. In 1980 the USDA had published a nutritional guidebook that warned eating large quantities of meat, eggs, dairy products, and sugar could endanger health. Farmers, especially cattleraisers, maintained that the Agriculture Department existed to serve the interests of food producers, that Bergland had let hostile consumer representatives take over the department, that the American people resented being told what they should eat, and that efforts to restrict established food additives and to expand labeling information were unnecessary and expensive.

Senator Roger Jepsen (a Republican from Iowa) told Block, "I shared with folks across this country when your nomination was submitted the idea that we truly would have a representative that does understand that the 'A' in 'USDA' stands for 'Agriculture' not 'U.S. Department of Consumerism' and not 'U.S. Department of Harassment,' but 'Agriculture.'"

When Senator David Pryor (a Democrat from Arkansas) asked how he differed philosophically from Bergland, Block said, "I strongly support the role of the Secretary of Agriculture serving as a strong advocate for the agriculture industry. I do not say that out of neglect for the consumer, because I think that is the best way I can serve the consumers of this country."

Senator S. I. Hayakawa (a Republican from California) complained about Bergland's support of "movements . . . led by Cesar Chavez and . . . the People's Republic of Berkeley to fight against mechanized harvesting of tomatoes." Block reassured him: "I strongly support research for improved agricultural production to include mechanization of our planting, harvesting, and tending processes. I have been in China . . . and seen a country where most of the people are on the land and, without some progress in mechanization we could be there today. Food would be much more expensive."

Commenting on the USDA's nutritional guidelines, Block said, "Hogs are just like people. You can provide protein and grain to a hog and he will balance his ration. He will eat about the right amount of protein to go along with the grain. People are surely as smart as hogs . . . I am not so sure that Government needs to get so deeply into telling people what they should and should not eat."

Block satisfied the senators' concerns by making appointments and by reorganizing the department to reestablish producers' dominance. He chose as his deputy Richard E. Lyng, a former president of the American Meat Institute, and as his assistant secretary for marketing C. W. McMillan, a lobbyist for the National Cattlemen's Association. He eliminated special offices for environmental quality and human nutrition. He also pleased Chair Jesse Helms and others on the Senate Agriculture Committee by his willingness to reduce food-stamp and other nutritional programs.

Food stamps had been controversial at the USDA largely because the program had expanded rapidly; its cost had increased from $36 million in 1965, when it served 424,000 people, to $11 billion in 1981, when it served 23 million.

Several senators on the Agriculture Committee believed their efforts to increase farm programs were hurt because of food stamps, which did not directly benefit farmers. All nutritional programs, including food stamps, cost a total of $16.2 billion; the entire USDA budget for 1981 was $26 billion. Even though the agency spent only $5.6 billion on assistance for farmers, these senators said, the public mistakenly believed that the Agriculture Department spent most of its money on farmers.

Food stamps had been created as an experimental method of distributing surplus commodities. The idea was to give poor people money good only to buy domestically produced food, which they could use in stores and supermarkets. This plan would deplete the surpluses more rapidly and at a lower administrative cost than other programs in which the government directly acquired and distributed food. The poor were chosen as beneficiaries because they were not then consuming much of the country's relatively expensive meat, poultry, and dairy products. Food stamps created a new source of demand—the millions of recipients. The increased demand helped farmers by raising prices, and it also reduced the need for more expensive farm programs. For years providing food to the hungry was a secondary goal of the food-stamp program under both Democratic and Republican secretaries of agriculture.

When Earl Butz successfully eliminated agricultural surpluses in 1972, he and others argued that farmers no longer needed food stamps and other nutritional programs, which then existed only to provide income for and improve the health of poor people. In short they had become welfare programs and as such should be transferred to the Department of Health, Education, and Welfare (HEW).

Few people doubted that it would be more logical for HEW to administer the food-stamps program, but liberals believed that because HEW was consistently under attack for being too expensive, transferring the program would make it more vulnerable to budget reductions. Many congressional farm leaders also opposed the transfer, because food stamps attracted the urban votes needed to pass farm legislation. By the time Butz left office, however, surpluses were building again. Some farm legislators argued that, once again, helping the poor buy food helped the farmer. Others, such as Senator Jesse Helms, were not convinced.

By 1977 several senators were angry because high-level officials in Bergland's department told the Agriculture Committee that the USDA should spend less for farm programs and more for food stamps. When Carl Curtis and others wanted to do just the opposite, they were frustrated.

Curtis said that the "individual lobbyists for . . . hunger groups" who currently occupied the "high spots in the Department of Agriculture" objected to his efforts to increase target prices and loan rates. "I have always been rather moderate in my belief about price supports," Curtis said. "But what I object to is turning the Department of Agriculture over to the nonagricultural interests, zooming the expenses by billions of dollars that have nothing to do with agricultural stability or prices and then zeroing in on the small 30 percent of the bill [benefiting farmers] and threatening a veto." Throughout Bergland's tenure farmers repeatedly pleaded intensely for congressional assistance; Curtis, Helms and others increased their attack on nutritional programs by arguing that the programs were wasteful and full of fraud.

During John Block's confirmation hearings in 1981 Helms became anxious when Block appeared to moderate his opposition to food stamps. Patrick Leahy (a Democrat from Vermont) got Block to admit that his previously quoted estimates of 40 percent waste in food stamps "has to be quite an exaggeration." Chair Helms then required Block to commit himself publicly to Helms' side:

"The CHAIRMAN. Mr. Secretary, is it fair to say that neither you nor I know the extent of abuse, fraud, and waste in the food stamp program?

"Mr. BLOCK. That is fair to say. I know we do not know.

"The CHAIRMAN. Is it fair to say that we have heard various credible estimates, ranging from 10 to 40 percent?

"Mr. BLOCK. We have heard that, sir.

"The CHAIRMAN. Right. Is it fair to say that we, meaning you as head of the Agriculture Department, and we as Senators, have a duty to the American people to determine what is the extent of the waste, abuse, and fraud, and eliminate it from the Federal budget?

"Mr. BLOCK. Yes sir, that would be our duty."

Helms and other committee members were later pleased when the Agriculture Department vigorously lobbied to cut nutritional programs, as it had under Butz. In 1981 Block's department proposed cutting $6 billion from food stamps over three years. The Agriculture Department succeeded in reducing not only the rate of growth but the actual cost of the program itself, a remarkable political accomplishment during a recession when unemployment was at its highest since the 1940s.

Helms's committee was also concerned about the secretary of agriculture's decline in power. Charles L. Frazier of the National Farmers Organization testified, "I should like to . . . encourage you, Mr. Chairman, Senator Huddleston, the committee to exercise your very considerable power in this town to bring back to the Secretary of Agriculture some of the authority that is granted him by law, but that has been pretty well spread around over town in recent administrations."

Senator David L. Boren (a Republican from Oklahoma) said about Bergland, "There are some of us who had the feeling that the current Secretary of Agriculture came to his post with good intentions; that he was sympathetic to the needs of the agriculture community. . . . Yet, somehow along the way, his voice did not seem to be heard. We had the feeling that even the decision on the embargo, perhaps, was not his own. Many, many other decisions appear to have been taken, really, without his full input."

Senator Mark Andrews (a Republican from North Dakota) told Block, "My colleague from Oklahoma pointed out the problems that my close friend and fellow farm producer had, because the White House did not let him run the Department of Agriculture as he should have run it. Bob Bergland is one of the finest men we have ever seen or will ever see as Secretary of Agriculture. I think you will be just as fine from the standpoint of the producers, and I only hope that the White House will give you the opportunity that Bob Bergland did not have to fight for farmers the way they should be stood up for."

John Melcher (a Democrat from Montana) said, "I would hope that you are going to set agricultural policy, not the Council of Economic Advisors, not the Office of Management and Budget, and not the new State Department. . . . Have you thought about this and have you discussed with President-elect Reagan as to whether you are going to run the show. . . . ?" Block was even asked, "If you find yourself in the position of being undercut by the White House and being outgunned by other departments of Government so that you feel that the vast majority of your policy recommendations in regard to agricultural issues are not being followed, what would you do about it?"

Block tried to answer the questions. He said, "I will be a strong voice and a strong advocate of agriculture, and I do not intend to take a second seat to other members of the Cabinet." He said, "I read the testimony of Secretary Bergland and the questions of this committee, and I know that things have not gone the way you had hoped. . . . Now, you ask if things went completely to pieces and we were not listened to. I am sure that there could be a time, under the most adverse conditions, that a Secretary would throw in the towel and say, 'I have done all I can do and we are not getting the job done.' I do not anticipate this, because I start off with great optimism and great purpose."

The committee, however, had asked the wrong person to provide assurances. Only President Reagan knew whether he intended to listen to his secretary of agriculture, and he wasn't testifying. As it turned out, Block's power to make agricultural policy decisions appeared to be even more limited than Bergland's. A profile of Block in the 1982 *Current Biography*, which rarely points out weak spots, noted, "Because of his mild manners, affability, and low-keyed charm, some veteran Washington observers have wondered whether Block can function effectively in the sparring ring of Capitol Hill politics, where no holds are barred." The influential and conservative Heritage Foundation said, "farm policy is not under the direction of the Secretary of Agriculture." Block functioned as a figurehead, representing U.S. agriculture during frequent trips abroad while other people made the significant policy decisions. By 1983 Block's official biography noted, "As an advocate of free trade, Block had visited 21 nations, both to protect existing markets and to lay groundwork for new markets."

Block left the day-to-day running of the department to his subordinates. Agencies the size of the USDA required considerable delegation because secretaries spent large chunks of time testifying before congressional committees, speaking before constituent groups, and talking to the press. These efforts were often essential to maintain critical support, but they also took away from the time a secretary devoted to getting things done. Effective secretaries generally carefully balanced their attention so they were in charge on issues within their own departments, or at least knew what their subordinates were doing. Equally important in Washington, they were *perceived* to be in charge. Bergland had not been perceived to be in charge, and there were reports that Howard W. Hjort, the USDA's chief economist, actually ran the department.

People perceived Block to have even less authority, in part because he played a negligible role in formulating the 1981 farm bill. He was often out of the country. The department's daily affairs were reportedly run by Deputy Lyng and William G. Lesher, the department's chief economist and the architect of both the 1981 farm bill and the 1982–83 Payment in Kind program.

As had happened four years earlier, the circumstances behind the farm bill's renewal weakened the president's ability to formulate agricultural policy. Early in 1981 President Reagan reduced his own effectiveness because Congress understood that he had given the secretary of agriculture limited authority. It was difficult for the administration to lead when its agricultural policy-makers, such as Budget Director David Stockman and other White House officials, worked on the issues only parttime, regarded agriculture as less important than their other duties, and could not take a public role. Nor did it help influence Congress that the secretary of agriculture frequently delegated his limited authority to subordinates.

In 1977, when the president had not taken the lead, the chairs of the Senate and House agriculture committees took over. In 1981, however, there were two new chairs, both of whom were weak and inexperienced.

Jesse Helms became chair of the Senate Agriculture Committee because in 1980 twelve Republican senators had been elected unexpectedly; one defeated Herman Talmadge. For the first time in twenty years the Republicans controlled the Senate and therefore had the committee chairs. As Senator Dole frequently reminded his colleagues, the rules for being in control were different. No longer could Republicans luxuriate in the traditional minority role of criticizing how the Senate was run. Also, because there was a Republican president, the Republican Senate had to try to cooperate with its party's president to run the country. To help to do so, senators, especially chairs, had to put together coalitions—a slow process frequently requiring that a person compromise long-held beliefs to get necessary legislation passed.

In 1981 Jesse Helms had become a national figure because he refused to compromise long-held positions. He was against abortion, unions, school busing, detente with the Russians, welfare, and deficit spending. He was for prayer in schools, support of Taiwan, and the right to carry handguns. He said, "Somewhere, somehow, the public must learn that it's of small importance whether [one] has charisma or glamour. The paramount thing is whether a man believes in the principles of America and whether he is willing to stand up for them, win or lose." In 1981 the liberal Americans for Democratic Action gave him a zero rating; the conservative Chamber of Commerce gave him 100 percent.

His power in Washington was based on close ties to President Reagan and his ability to raise large sums of money. Back in 1976, when Reagan was trying to take the nomination away from President Ford, Helms secured an important early victory for Reagan in North Carolina's primary. The president believed Helms's role as a key advisor in the 1980 campaign had helped him get elected.

Helms's extensive direct-mail solicitations were often cited as an example of the New Right's power. His 1978 reelection in North Carolina had been one of the most expensive senatorial campaigns ever waged, and he raised more than $6 million. Then he developed a warchest independent of the Republican Party and solely under his control. By 1982 his Congressional Club had raised some $10 million to spend on conservative candidates and causes.

Helms did not consider it necessary to subordinate his views to those of the less conservative Republican leaders in the Senate. Nor was he interested in concentrating primarily on agricultural issues the way his predecessor had done. Herman Talmadge had reportedly traded his vote on the Panama Canal Treaty for time to consider farm legislation on the floor of the Senate. He had repeatedly subordinated his personal views to advance the work of his committee, but it was inconceivable that Jesse Helms would even consider compromising his position on an important foreign-policy issue. In fact early in 1981 Helms took considerable time away from his duties as chair of the Agriculture Committee to delay confirmation of Reagan's appointees to the State Department, whose views he considered insufficiently conservative.

Because Helms was so consistently uncompromising, he offended many congressional colleagues, including those who agreed with him. He later tried but failed to obtain Senate approval for measures that would have made abortion, school busing, and prohibiting prayer in public schools unconstitutional. Many senators voted against him simply because they did not like his disruptive tactics.

Helms also did not have much interest in agricultural issues; the only programs that concerned him were tobacco and peanuts, important industries in his state of North Carolina. During markup on the farm bill for 1981, the *Congressional Quarterly* noted, Helms demanded that his fellow committee members compromise, but he refused to reciprocate. "More than once Chairman Helms warned members that they would have to 'march back down the hill' — that is, reduce the cost of programs — before reporting a bill. 'We've already broken the bank,' Helms said. . . . Then, acknowledging to committee members that he, too, had his 'special interests,' Helms sat quietly while the committee endorsed his proposal to retain the peanut program without the changes that Reagan requested."

His personal unpopularity made him vulnerable to attack on other issues and eroded existing legislative support for tobacco and peanuts. Representatives explained on the floor of the House that they refused to vote for a bill that would help Jesse Helms.

Later, when Helms asked Congress to implement the president's Payment in Kind Program (PIK) for 1982, there was general support for PIK but the Senate refused Helms's request for floor time to vote on the legislation. An indignant Senator Paul E. Tsongas (a Democrat from Massachusetts) explained that even though he supported the bill, "I will not participate in anything that rewards Helms." In 1981 Senate Majority Leader Howard Baker (a Republican from Tennessee) decided Helms could not be trusted to carry the farm bill. It was highly unusual to ask a senator to bail out a committee chair who had alienated so many of his colleagues, but Baker asked Bob Dole, chair of the Finance Committee, to secure the balanced support the farm bill for 1981 needed to make it through the Senate.

Meanwhile, in the House, E. (Kika) de la Garza (a Democrat from Texas), the new chair of the Agriculture Committee, was having problems of his own. Previous Chair Tom Foley had become minority whip, an important post, especially since the House was now the only body of Congress the Democrats controlled. De la Garza's elevation to the chair apparently caught him unprepared. The respected *Almanac of American Politics* observed, "No one claims de la Garza is a vastly original thinker."

Although de la Garza later won respect from committee and congressional colleagues, in 1981 he wasn't familiar with the major agricultural issues outside of his Fifteenth District in southern Texas. He also wasn't prepared for the complicated budget and political issues that made 1981 the most difficult year ever to pass omnibus farm legislation.

Two years later de la Garza described what he learned from the experience. "Whatever Congress does about commodity supports in the next farm bill will be controversial, and it won't be done easily. Some of you may remember that the Conference Report on the 1981 farm bill passed the House by a margin of just two votes. I hope that we can get enough agreement to get a better margin on the next bill, but anyone who thinks it's going to be easy is just fooling himself."

In 1981 de la Garza relied on his strong subcommittee chairs to specify provisions and language for issues related to their highly technical specialties. But when the subcommittees brought back unacceptably expensive sections, there wasn't enough time to reach a satisfactory compromise with the different constituents. De la Garza later recommended avoiding a repetition of the process: "If . . . farmers are going to have a chance to make their plans efficiently, they have to get the word on the . . . government programs as soon as possible before they plant. . . . We know that there are going to be some disagreements about what the next general farm law should provide. . . . [W]e have to . . . get all the issues out on the table for study and for thorough discussion . . . and then we have to sit down to find out if we can find reasonable and practical ways to produce programs which will serve the needs of farmers, . . . consumers and tax payers. . . . [W]e could save a lot of time."

In 1981 de la Garza did not have that time. When the technicalities of the budget process helped make the bill too complicated for him to handle, Democratic leaders asked Tom Foley to step in and help save it. As a result the real leaders of the farm bills in both House and Senate, were other people than the agriculture committee chairs. In the past Congress's internal problems could have been corrected privately, but by 1981 the press regularly reported that de la Garza and Helms were not in charge. These reports encouraged the farm bill's opponents to believe they might be successful. They almost were, after a series of divisive actions split the old coalition that traditionally united to pass farm bills.

The farm community was divided within itself because the budget process restricted the total funds available for agricultural programs.[1] The cost of the dairy program alone had unexpectedly skyrocketed to more than $2 billion in fiscal 1981, more than the Senate Budget Committee wanted to spend on all farm programs together. Although the dairy sector was small compared to the total farm economy, its political action committees spent large sums supporting the election campaigns of key representatives and senators, so the dairy people had significant power in Congress. Nevertheless when the grain interests fought the dairy interests during consideration of the bill, the dairy interests were set back. They had a hard time defending additional assistance when the USDA was already purchasing and storing millions of pounds of milk, cheese, and non-fat dry milk. In March 1981, USDA's inventory of dairy products was 973 million pounds, which increased to 1.6 billion pounds by the end of the year. Because of various conflicts in the agricultural community, angry members of the congressional farm block refused to support the committee's final bill.

Meanwhile many urban- and suburban-based representatives had difficulty voting for a bill with large cuts in food stamps. (The savings were applied to farm programs.) Even after the House and Senate passed bills and the conference committee had agreed on a compromise, the bill's opponents persevered. It was generally routine for both houses to approve the final version of legislation the conference had worked out, but in this case the House of Representatives nearly scuttled almost a year's worth of work.

The bill cleared the House by two votes, which meant that one changed vote would have blocked passage. De la Garza later told a story about how he secured the essential vote: on December 16, 1981, it had been chaotic in the well of the House. De la Garza buttonholed many of the representatives who were milling around. Desperate, he approached a representative from California who he knew did not have any interest in farm legislation. The representative surprisingly agreed to vote for the bill. "I dared not kiss him on the floor," de la Garza later said.

When the vote was over, de la Garza asked the California representative why he had voted for the bill. "I don't know about your damn farm program. I gave you my vote because I hate to see a grown man cry." After he told the story, de la Garza observed, "That's how we passed the '81 farm bill."

In 1981 the administration and Congress became so distracted by the process of creating legislation that they failed to understand the basic transformation taking place in the farm economy. Suddenly inflation was disappearing. In 1980 the inflation rate had been 12.4 percent, the second year in a row of double-digit inflation in the longest period of inflation since World War I. By 1981 the rate was down to 8.9 percent. After record declines in some items' prices, the rate was down to 3.9 percent in 1982, 3.8 percent in 1983, and 4 percent in 1984. The rapid move from inflation to disinflation surprised economists and even the Reagan administration officials who took credit for it. It threatened to devastate farmers.

Farmers had profited from inflation. In 1979 the average farm family earned more than $27,000, its highest income in history. During the 1970s net farm income reached record rates, and for the first time ever farmers had higher personal disposable incomes than the general population. In 1979 net farm income was $32.3 billion, $5.6 billion more than the previous year; after subtracting the effects of inflation, it was an increase of $1.3 billion in real dollars.

These high incomes were a result of high prices, big crops, and increased exports. In September 1980 wheat on the Chicago Board of Trade sold for $5.23 a bushel, and corn was $3.70—the highest prices ever and a dramatic increase from the $1.44 wheat and $1.22 corn in 1971. Farmers were growing record crops; they produced 1 billion more bushels of wheat in 1980 than in 1970. Because the country needed less than 800 million bushels for domestic use, most of the

2.4-billion-bushel wheat crop went for export. In 1980 farmers sold three times more grain abroad than ten years earlier.

They also went into record debt. From 1971 to 1981 farmers' real-estate debt more than tripled. By 1981 farmers had borrowed more than $91 billion mortgaging their farms to grow more crops to earn more money. From 1970 to 1980 production costs not including land increased more than two and a half times, largely because petroleum prices had skyrocketed. Petroleum was the largest single raw material used in farming; it not only ran tractors, airplanes, combines, and other machinery, but it was an important ingredient in chemical fertilizers and other products. Despite rising costs farmers used 37 percent more chemicals on farmland in 1980 than in 1970.

During that decade farmers were willing to do everything possible to increase production, and bankers were willing to help them both because commodity prices were high and because the land itself seemed extremely valuable. From 1970 to 1980 the average cost of an acre of farmland in Iowa increased from $392 to $1811. The prices of land defied economic sense if one assumed that prices for wheat, corn, and soybeans would stay at the same level. Even a wheat farmer who received the high 1980 price of $5.23 a bushel would have difficulty paying $1811 per acre. In 1978 a concerned House Agriculture Committee noted that "farmland in the United States has had more value as a speculative investment than as a means of production."

The high costs could be explained if one assumed a dramatic increase in prices for commodities, or if food suddenly became difficult to obtain. During the 1970s both assumptions seemed plausible, and as late as 1980 farmers argued that a bushel of wheat should be considered as valuable as a barrel of oil, then selling for $35. Investors argued that during rapid inflation, when the dollar was becoming less valuable, no matter how much one paid for an acre, the price was likely to go up later because no new farmland was being created.

Another factor was that because the dollar was weak, real estate was less expensive for people with foreign currency. Throughout the 1970s there were reports that farmland in the United States was being taken over by foreign purchasers. The extent of foreign investment was exaggerated. Each year less than 3 percent of the total acreage was for sale, and the General Accounting Office found in 1979 that foreign buyers acquired only 8 percent of the 3 percent. They did, however, help increase the cost of land, and the principal beneficiaries were the farmers themselves.

As real-estate values skyrocketed, so did farmers' personal wealth; some became paper millionaires virtually overnight. From 1970 to 1980 farmers' assets increased from $271 billion to $905 billion. Since most farmers owned their own land, they did not have to factor that cost into their planting decisions. For most, the problem of paying for $1811-per-acre land with $5.23 (or less)-per-bushel wheat was hypothetical. Instead the increased value of their land increased their ability to borrow. Bankers were willing to increase mortgages because they believed land was good collatoral. Even if a farmer defaulted, it would be easy to sell off the farm at a profit.

The increased mortgages helped increase spending power. Farmers put more fertilizer on the land, increasing productivity per acre of wheat by three bushels from 1970 to 1979. They also bought expensive equipment and more land. Because the general farm economy was doing well and income was increasing, bankers were also willing to make unsecured loans for operating expenses. From 1970 to 1980 non-real-estate farm debt increased from $16 billion to $60 billion.

Most farmers benefited, but not all. The unexpected prosperity that hit the farm community in 1972 and continued despite interruptions for nearly a decade encouraged people to enter farming. The new farmers bought and leased land and equipment at high prices, and they found themselves in financial distress. Wheat prices dropped from $4.94 in 1973 to $2.59 in 1977 before going back up again, and the disappointed new farmers became the nucleus of grassroots protests. Late in 1977 they formed a loosely organized ad hoc group composed largely of grain and cotton producers called the American Agriculture Movement (AAM). AAM called for a strike, which farmers ignored, to raise prices by withholding crops from market and land from production. They also demanded that the government pass legislation to make it "illegal for anyone to buy, sell or trade any agricultural product at less than 100 percent of parity."

Parity was a technical term. It referred to a scale that balanced the price of farm products (including interest, wages, and taxes) with the price of consumer items. For example during an established base year a farmer might be able to buy one pair of overalls with the proceeds from one bushel of wheat. If the price of wheat dropped in the following year so two bushels had to be sold to buy the overalls, then wheat would be selling for 50 percent of parity.

By law the Department of Agriculture based its parity figures on market prices from 1910 to 1914. During that pre-World War I period farm prices were unusually high, which was why New Deal populists institutionalized it as a base. By the 1970s and '80s productivity had increased dramatically. For a variety of political reasons, however, the base remained the same even though parity had become an unrealistic gauge of farm prosperity.

The USDA, which figures out the parity rate, had little practical use for it except in programs for a few commodities such as milk, tobacco, and peanuts, which Earl Butz had not been able to change. Butz's legislative reform, however, had released most cropland from the parity-based system that used allotments. Farm legislators decided it was difficult to defend a system of payments that involved extensive government control of land and was based on a pre-World War I formula. Even after Butz left, Congress retained the newly created mechanism of target prices and loan rates.

Nevertheless the word *parity* had rhetorical power. For farmers in economic distress it symbolized an age when government cared, and the AAM used *parity* as a rallying cry that stood for equality. When protesting farmers arrived in Washington to lobby for guaranteed *parity*, they were ambiguous about its meaning. For some, 100-percent parity meant using the 1910 to 1914 formula; for others it meant a less clearly defined price that included production costs plus a reasonable profit.

AAM spokespeople used the second meaning in their legislative proposals, which legislators and established farmers' groups predicted would fail. Chair Talmadge, for example, said, "We would like to get better supports for farmers, but it's a question of what can be done and until you change public opinion around and then turn votes in Congress around, there's little hope. At least half the representatives in Congress have no farmers in their districts and they aren't inclined to spend more of the Government's money to help." Chair Foley said, "I have an open mind on this. But the cost of the current program they are complaining about is so great that we're already hitting opposition from nonfarm representatives. It would be hard to get anything more."

The protesting farmers surprised Congress with their tenacity. They spent months in Washington tying up rush-hour traffic, releasing goats on the Capitol steps, and taking over an office at the Department of Agriculture. Legislators found it impossible to avoid the farmers, who buttonholed representatives in the hallways, filled hearing rooms with testimony, parked enormous tractors along the mall, and were clearly present in local restaurants and hotels. Diana McLellan, the gossip columnist for *The Washington Star*, said their tastes were expensive, and they drank up all the available Perrier water in Capitol Hill bars.

The farmers were successful. Chair Foley said that the AAM's protests had created "a climate in which we can do something for farmers." In 1978, less than a year after enacting the 1977 farm law, both houses passed a major farm bill that the Carter administration predicted would raise food prices by 3 percent, would cost the government as much as $9 billion in payments, and "would be one of the most inflationary actions of the federal government in recent years." For various reasons, some technical and some political, no final bill reached the president's desk. Nevertheless the government increased target prices and loan rates, declared a moratorium on foreclosures of Farmers Home Administration loans, created new low-cost "economic emergency" loans, and established a new grain-reserve program.

The AAM farmers had convinced Congress that inflation endangered the agricultural economy by forcing farmers to increase their debt to pay for higher production costs, whenever the increased prices for their products lagged behind. Farmers, they said, were stuck in an inflationary spiral: every year they put themselves in worse financial shape but could not stop selling their necessarily larger crops for less than production costs because they needed the income to pay for land, equipment, production, and debt.

Congress did not understand that in 1978, the year of AAM's greatest success, most farmers benefited from inflation. Their net income from the farms and per capita disposable income jumped to the second-highest levels in history. Their prosperity was real because most of them owned their own land. As long as prices continued to rise, which they did for two years beginning in 1978, then crop sizes increased, exports expanded, and most farmers made money. Even the farmers who did not benefit wanted inflation to continue. They had purchased expensive land and had gone heavily into debt, hoping the increased prices for their crops and land would be even higher at some point in the future. Although they opposed paying more for fertilizer and other goods, they depended on inflated prices to stay in business and eventually earn a profit. Inflation related only to expenses. Farmers did not regard high prices for commodities as inflationary, because they believed that given their expenses, their prices were less than they deserved. From 1970 to 1980 farmers' gross sales increased from $35 billion to $81 billion. Even though consumers' food costs more than doubled during this period, and increased food costs led the rise in the general inflation rate, farmers argued that their prices had been too low for years. They said that even though it was more expensive, America's food was still a bargain compared to what people paid in other countries. Although many farmers were middlemen themselves as members of agricultural cooperatives, they complained that most of the money from increased consumers' costs went not to farmers, but to the middlemen who processed, packaged, transported, and sold the food.

Congressional agricultural leaders were frightened by the prospect of an inflation-based disaster. Donald Patterson, a delegate to the AAM from Virginia, wrote in *The New York Times:* "The critical national need right now is to restore income to the agricultural economy before circumstances become any worse. If foreclosures continue at an accelerating rate, other farm loans will be called into question. As farms fail, so will rural banks and other rural businesses. From there the process will spread to larger banks and on through the economy." Congressional agricultural leaders persuaded their colleagues in 1978, as they had in 1977, to pass programs intended to protect farmers against inflation by keeping farm prices high, although the assistance was not as much as farmers wanted. The representatives believed that as long as target prices and loan rates did not guarantee a profit, then they were not inflationary and didn't stimulate unnecessary production for government warehouses.

There were problems, however, with using target prices and loan rates to implement agricultural policy. Because it was difficult to estimate reliably what farmers actually paid for production costs, the higher price supports continued to provide a profit to some farmers while not covering others' costs. The parity formula for cotton and grain had at least been precise, even though it had institutionalized an out-of-date base period.

For most farmers the higher price supports had limited effect. For the largest farmers, who produced most of the country's food, the payment limitation of $50,000 was too low to do much good. During years of acreage set-asides, the requirement that farmers participate to receive benefits caused many large farmers to ignore entirely the government's farm programs, as the disappointingly low participation in the 1979 set-aside indicated. Many farmers with small and medium-sized operations had protected themselves from the vicissitudes of the farm economy by getting jobs and farming parttime. Throughout the 1970s the statistics on farmers' income included revenue from "off farm" jobs that was consistently higher than from farming. The principal beneficiaries of the governmental programs appeared to be inefficient producers, who got low yields per acre, and whose relatively high holdings of marginally productive land made it attractive to leave acreage idle.

Congressional farm leaders panicked and acted because they didn't have timely information for making decisions. Despite their initial unwillingness even to consider legislation less than a year after enacting the 1977 omnibus farm law, in 1978 they ended up increasing farm payments when the figures showed that farmers' prosperity was reaching record highs. But figures for net farm income and farmers' per capita disposable income were not precise enough for policy-making. If some farmers really were in distress, no existing figures pinpointed the degree of danger and its likely effect on the whole farm economy. Congress had to rely on the testimony of the people most likely to benefit from exaggerating their problems.

Thus Congress had no effective way to determine which farmers needed assistance, how much they needed, and how to make sure they received it. By 1981 the entire system of agriculture and food production, including farming, food processing, resource supplies, manufacturing, transportation, wholesaling, retailing, and restaurants, generated 20 percent of the gross national product and 22 percent of the nation's jobs. Agricultural exports were the largest single source of foreign exchange, in recent years offsetting as much as 50 percent of the cost of importing petroleum. Agriculture was too important for legislators to err by giving farmers too little, even when they recognized that doing otherwise might be inefficient and expensive.

In 1981, when Congress was again considering major legislation, most experts agreed inflation was farmers' biggest problem. In the *Annual Report of the Council of Economic Advisors* the outgoing Carter administration said, "Finding new and more flexible ways to use resources more efficiently while guarding against price volatility will be the principal farm policy challenge of the 1980s." John Block put it more simply at his confirmation hearings. "This has to be priority No. 1 with me, to do what I can in my capacity as Secretary of Agriculture to help improve the profitability of farming . . . I think . . . the first item of business has to be getting inflation under control." Jesse Helms said, "Farmers understand that unless this inflation is reduced, they don't stand a chance no matter what kind of farm bill we pass."

The four-year farm bill President Reagan signed on December 22, 1981, set a minimum loan rate for wheat at $3.55 per bushel and a target price of $4.05, to increase to $4.65 by 1985. This and the prices for corn, cotton, and other commodities were regarded as modest protection for farmers. Agriculture Department officials assumed that inflation would continue at double-digit rates despite the administration's efforts. Assistant Agriculture Secretary Lesher later explained that "the 1981 Farm Bill that was eventually signed . . . appeared workable" because it "contained provisions for higher loan rate minimums . . . and annual target price increases of 3 to 5 percent. . . . It seemed to represent an effective compromise between our [the Reagan administration's] initial bill and the signed Farm Bill that many in Congress viewed as containing support levels that were much too low. . . . [T]he closeness of the vote was because it provided too *little* to farmers and not too much. Indeed, many in the Congress and elsewhere called it a 'do nothing' bill for farmers."

Back in May 1981 prices for wheat on the Chicago Board of Trade had dropped to $4.60 per bushel, down from the 1980 price of $5.23. Many observers regarded the drop as a temporary aberration, not realizing that farm and food prices fell first when the inflationary period ended, just as they had risen first when it began. By 1982, when prices dropped to $3.69 in Chicago and lower still for farmers selling cash wheat to their local grain elevator, the government's price supports were higher than market prices. In fact farmers' income supports were growing faster than the inflation rate. By 1983 Lesher and other USDA officials were asking Congress to cancel scheduled increases for income supports. They said they had been mistaken, that the 1981 act they had believed was anti-inflationary was actually promoting inflation.

The 1981 law significantly expanded the government's grain-reserve programs. One provision let the secretary of agriculture acquire a minimum of 1 billion bushels of feed grains and 700 million bushels of wheat. Congress and the administration both believed that if farmers found it attrac-

tive to store grain rather than sell it, they would be able
to use the marketplace more effectively. The theory was
that when export markets were expanding and worldwide
demand was expected to increase indefinitely, reserves acted
as a temporary buffer. If farmers could take more grain
out of the marketplace, prices would rise. When the expected additional world purchases took place, farmers would
have more grain to sell and could then reimburse the
government for the loans, thus significantly reducing the
cost of farm programs.

Instead in 1982 the world market declined unexpectedly
and dramatically. Between 1981 and 1983 exports fell nearly
12 percent, and the agricultural trade surplus dropped from
$26.6 billion to $18.6 billion. This country's share of world
agricultural trade declined from 61 percent in 1980 to 50
percent in 1983.

The decline in exports was partially a result of a strong
dollar, which made the United States' agricultural products
more expensive for foreign buyers. A weak dollar had been
partially responsible for the dramatic increase in
agricultural exports during the 1970s by making the United
States' products relatively inexpensive. Nevertheless the
Reagan administration worked to strengthen the dollar; it
was more successful than it would have liked. The theory
was that a weak dollar damaged international trade because
of its instability. Senator Charles H. Percy (a Republican
from Illinois) had said at Block's confirmation hearings that
one "responsibility" of the new secretary of agriculture was
"to strengthen the dollar."

Meanwhile weather conditions produced record crops
throughout the world, lowering demand. Foreign customers
were less able to buy because of a worldwide recession
coupled with financial crises in the developing world and
in centrally controlled economies such as the Soviet Union,
the export markets that had formerly grown well.
Simultaneously these customers were offered more attrac-

tive prices from the United States' competitors, who were expanding production, increasing export subsidies, and benefiting from the dollar's competitive disadvantage. They had also, unlike the embargo-prone United States, demonstrated their reliability to suppliers.

The export market's decline seemed to threaten U.S. farmers, who had dramatically expanded during the 1970s until a third of all their production went to foreign customers. Farmers thus depended on foreign sales for up to 30 percent of their income. Meanwhile the Reagan administration's efforts to slow inflation also produced a more severe recession than had been expected, lowering demand for food in this country even though prices were dropping rapidly.

The officials in the Agriculture Department had congratulated themselves on producing a modest 1981 farm bill in keeping with the Reagan administration's goals to limit the government's agricultural payments and controls. Instead, as Assistant Secretary Lesher—the bill's architect—later put it, "The farm bill . . . has become unworkable in almost lightning speed." Even though domestic and world markets were decreasing, the bill stimulated production by making it profitable to grow for government warehouses. By the end of 1982 the United States had acquired one of the largest surpluses in history. More than 66 percent of a year's wheat crop, 1.6 billion bushels, and more than 47 percent of a year's corn crop, 3.4 billion bushels, were in storage. Despite these enormous reserves farmers were producing grain at record levels even though there was no place to put it; storage bins were filled to capacity, and the marketplace didn't need more.

When President Reagan signed the 1981 farm bill, the government was spending $4 billion on farm programs. The Reagan administration believed the new legislation would save money. In 1982 Assistant Secretary Lesher testified, "As the chief economist of the Department of Agriculture,

I feel bad that the estimates were so far off the mark. . . . [P]eople will criticize me because I estimated $1.8 billion in cost this year for the farm programs and now all of a sudden it's turned out to be close to $12 billion. What kind of credibility do I have? What kind of credibility does the Department have?"

By 1982 the Agriculture Department's primary problem was not how to avoid even higher government payments, which were unavoidable, but how to prevent a catastrophe in the agricultural economy. In 1982 Representative Berkley Bedell (a Democrat from Iowa) told Congress, "I know members have heard time after time about the problems of our farmers. Let me tell them, this time our farmers really have problems."

Early in 1982 the estimates for net farm income had dropped so low the Agriculture Department stopped publishing them. Senator Alan Dixon (a Democrat from Illinois) introduced legislation requiring the secretary of agriculture to continue publishing the statistics every month. He said, "The level of farm income is an important indicator of the health of rural America. The level of farm income helps Congress to evaluate whether or not legislative action is required to preserve our vital food and fiber producing industry, an industry that contributes more to our balance of payments than any other. It is intolerable that we in Congress should be denied the information available to the Secretary of Agriculture."

Secretary Block argued that net farm income was not a reliable indicator of what was taking place in the agricultural sector. "The sector has simply become too diverse, too complex, and too dynamic to be prematurely assessed on the basis of a single aggregate statistic which relies on a limited data base."

Witnesses testifying before a subcommittee of the Senate Agriculture Committee agreed that using net farm income had limitations, but at least it indicated what was happening in the farm economy; Reagan's budget cutbacks were making it harder to obtain information. Raymond Daniel, an agricultural economist for Chase Econometrics, said, "The Secretary . . . wants to shoot the messenger of—the carrier of bad news." Agricultural economist J. B. Penn said, "I think that if a return to more prosperous times in the farm sector were in the offing in 1984 that this administration would probably have a much different view about dissemination of forecasts of improved farm income." He also observed, "The Department of Agriculture has a long tradition of providing reliable, objective, and comprehensive statistics and research studies on American agriculture and the food system. Those functions have continued through the years in both Democratic and Republican Administrations, and by and large remained free of taint. More recently, however, a growing number of people are seeing reasons for serious concern. The budget for these functions has been eroding over the years, and quite significantly in the current fiscally austere climate. And, more and more reports are being heard of suppressed studies and of estimates having to pass political as well as professional muster before being issued. The value of this system, above all, is its credibility—if this is undermined, the system loses all value."

The administration released its figures, but it delayed until farmers received a $4-billion advance on their governmental payments before the November Congressional elections, much as they had received advances before the Congressional elections of 1978. The estimate was that in 1982 net farm income was $19 billion, a significant drop from $25 billion in the previous year.

One reason for the delay was to avoid panic. The figures for net farm income, adjusted for the effects of inflation, were lower than during the Depression. USDA officials correctly observed that this comparison did not take into account the decline from 6.5 million farmers in the 1930s to

2.5 million. Assistant Secretary Lesher, for example, noted, "Even after adjusting for inflation, real net income per farm is more than three times larger than in the 1930s." But real net income per farm was also declining. Although the USDA did not know the extent of the trouble, officials were very worried because there was a significant risk of a land bust.

In 1982, for the first time in more than twenty-five years, the value of farmland declined. No one knew how far it would fall. The agricultural economy had become dependent on high land costs. Even when prices for commodities were high and markets were expanding, the land costs had seemed excessive; in 1982, however, prices were down, and markets were contracting. Bankers were suddenly anxious. They had lent $216 billion to farmers, much of it based on real estate estimated to be worth $773 billion, and some of them predicted that as many as 25 percent of their farm clients would fail to qualify for refinancing. As loans became delinquent, bankers faced the prospect of foreclosing and acquiring land they would have difficulty selling even at a fraction of its paper value.

After what he called the "economic alarm" had subsided, W. D. Willer of the American Bankers Association said, "Commercial ag bankers and other ag lenders scrambled the first half of 1983 in various ways to keep their borrowers and themselves on an even keel. Lenders suggested partial liquidation in many instances. . . . As we move on in 1983 to midyear, it becomes more apparent that with the advent of partial liquidation of personal property, prices received for machinery and livestock are getting stickier and stickier. Also, land acres being offered for sale were increasing by the month, which stalemated sales in many areas, thus decreasing the possibility of debt reduction for those in trouble."

Some observers predicted that unless the government acted, the deteriorating farm economy with lowered land values, increased farm debt, and accelerated bankruptcies would cause bank failures, which in turn would seriously damage the U.S. economy as a whole. In September 1982 Senator Edward Zorinksy (a Republican from Nebraska) said in an appeal to Block, "Mr. Secretary, I ask you to consider seriously the consequences of failing to act in the current crisis. Consider both the human consequences and the implication for our entire national economy. . . . Don't let today's agricultural depression precipitate a 'farm led and farm fed' depression throughout the rest of the American economy."

USDA officials were particularly concerned about the people who owned the large farms that produced most of the country's food. In 1980 the 286,000 farmers whose operation sold $100,000 or more in farm products each year accounted for about 57 percent of all farm products sold and about 60 percent of the farm debt. They had leveraged their assets to borrow as much money as possible to expand their already large operations, to pay for operating expenses, and to buy large and expensive equipment. While farmers overall increased their ratio of debts to assets from 16 percent in 1970 to 21 percent by 1983, the large farmers' *average* ratio was more than 37 percent. Some went up to 70 percent. These farmers depended entirely on farming for their income, unlike most farmers, whose primary income came from elsewhere.

Large farmers could not depend on government programs to avoid disaster; the restrictions and limitations in the 1981 act were similar to the ones in the 1977 legislation. But because these farmers were so important to the agricultural economy, and because they were in so much financial danger, the USDA needed to help them as well as to limit their production. From 1979 to 1983 grain production had been at record highs, and continued large crops threatened to depress farm prices still more.

Secretary Block and other Reagan administration officials had said they did not believe in imposing production controls because the marketplace should control the agricultural economy. When Congress was considering the 1981 farm bill, they requested that Congress end the secretary's authority to take land out of production through set-asides. Six months later, in September 1981, Block announced a program to set aside 15 percent of the country's wheat land. In January 1982 he announced a 10 percent set-aside for corn and feedgrains. Congress considered these actions to be too little, too late.

After two straight years of last-minute set-asides, in 1983 Congress passed legislation requiring the secretary of agriculture to announce his intentions on a timely basis. Reagan vetoed it. House Agriculture Committee Chair Kika de la Garza told the story of two farmers talking about the USDA's set-aside program for the year: One farmer says, "I know the government hasn't announced its intentions. I haven't planted my crop yet."

In 1982 the set-aside programs had disappointingly low participation rates, 20 percent for corn and 48 percent for wheat. Even though the programs kept nearly 11 million acres of land from being planted, the wheat and corn crops in 1982 were larger than in 1981. Farmers increased their production per acre; wheat increased from an average of 36 to 40 bushels per acre in one year. The historic characteristic of acreage controls was that farmers took out of production their least productive land, which one observer described as "swamps . . . and sand dunes." Nevertheless the only power the secretary of agriculture had to control production was to control acreage. To work, the controls had to be so extensive that after taking millions of acres of less productive land out of production, farmers had no choice but to let productive farmland lie fallow as well.

Toward the end of 1982 USDA officials believed emergency action was necessary to save the farm economy. They knew that Congress was incapable of rapid action and that the 1981 farm bill had badly divided the farm community. In December 1981 Budget Director David Stockman revealed what had been his true motivations during the year: "My strategy is to come in with a farm bill that's unacceptable to the farm guys so that the whole thing begins to splinter." Throughout 1982 farm legislators read aloud to their colleagues this and other passages from Stockman's well-distributed *Atlantic Monthly* interview. The administration had helped create a farm bill that, less than a year later, defied all their predictions; at the same time congressional Democrats were denouncing cutbacks in the budget for the poor. The country was in the midst of a severe recession. It was not a good time to ask Congress for major new and expensive legislation to help farmers with operations that were large and, at least on paper, wealthy.

So USDA officials had to figure out how to help avert catastrophe while requiring little or no congressional action. In January 1983, in a speech before the American Farm Bureau Federation convention, President Reagan announced he was implementing a "payment in kind" (PIK) program, which he called a "crop swap." In 1982 Secretary Block had announced a 20 percent set-aside for wheat and others for corn and other crops. Farmers who not only signed up with these programs but also agreed to withhold another 10 to 30 percent of their land would be paid well for withholding the additional land. The government would pay wheat farmers 95 percent of their yield per acre, and other farmers would get 80 percent. But instead of being paid in money, they would be paid with crops from the grain and cotton in storage. PIK was designed to let as much as 50 percent of the nation's cropland lay idle — the largest acreage-control program ever. It also provided that some farmers could be paid to let their entire farm lie fallow.

The 1981 law limited payments to any one farmer to $50,000 and required that market prices reach an established minimum before the government could release its reserves. When Congress was unable to act on the proposed changes, however, despite strong sentiment that congressional approval was indeed necessary, USDA lawyers decided that it was legal to go ahead. In their view the limitations on payments and reserves related only to cash. The General Accounting Office later told Congress that PIK violated the law by allowing payments of more than $50,000, but by then the program was already being implemented.

By the end of 1983 the Agriculture Department had taken 80 million acres of land out of production. The program appeared to be surprisingly successful. In 1983 net farm income increased, and by September 1983 Chicago prices showed a recovery from the previous year. Wheat was up to $4.07 from $3.69, and corn was up to $3.66 from $2.49. Participation in PIK was estimated at 75 percent of the wheat farmers and 65 percent of the corn farmers. The USDA received unexpected assistance when the worst drought in fifty years hit the corn belt, further reducing supply. At a USDA conference in November 1983 Earl Butz quipped, "This year God signed up for PIK."

In less than a year the drought and acreage reductions took corn from dangerously high surpluses to end-of-the-year supplies so low that some observers worried there might be a shortage. The success for wheat was more limited. By the end of the year there were still 1.5 billion bushels in storage, although as Assistant Secretary Lesher pointed out, "without the PIK program ending stocks would have been a fifth larger."

The Reagan administration combined PIK with existing USDA programs to reduce reserves, cut production, and increase income. The action averted a short-term agricultural crisis, giving agricultural policy-makers time;

a new farm bill was up for consideration in 1985. But the cost was high.

Net payment to farmers increased from $2.8 billion in 1980 to $18.9 billion in 1983. The tab did not include the direct costs of the PIK program, which the General Accounting Office estimated might be an additional $11 billion. Although net payments to farmers declined to an estimated $6.2 billion in 1984, they were expected to increase to $11.5 billion in both 1985 and 1986. These costs embarrassed a Republican president who had promised to reduce government spending for agriculture and return farmers to a market-oriented economy.

Even worse than the budgetary situation was the growing belief that American agricultural policy had gone out of control. The secretary of agriculture seemed powerless to implement his objectives. Secretary Block boasted that PIK was "the most effective acreage reduction program in history," but in the same speech he said, "As a farmer myself, I can tell you that idling productive acreage is not an option the U.S. farmers prefer. American farmers pride themselves on their ability to produce, and they want their income from the marketplace—not the Treasury. Continued acreage adjustment programs are simply not the type of programs that a market-oriented agriculture needs."

Following the November 1984 election, the Reagan administration once again prepared for a four year farm bill by threatening to make massive cuts in farm spending. Secretary Block once again defended cuts, saying that farmers should stop depending on the government and use the free market as the guide to determine their income. Despite massive Soviet grain purchases in the summer of 1984, U.S. wheat farmers ended the year with 1.4 billion bushels in storage and a 1985 wheat crop estimated at 2.6 billion bushels.

In November 1984 Jesse Helms, who won reelection in the most expensive senate race in U.S. history, became eligible to chair the prestigious foreign relations committee. Nevertheless, he gave up the opportunity, keeping a promise made to his North Carolina constituents, and remained as head of the agriculture committee. The 1985 farm bill, he explained, was too important.

By 1985 congressional agricultural committee chairs were again divided over what the objectives of agricultural policy should be and were unable to unite the farm community, whose members were fighting among themselves for larger shares of government programs. They also did not have the leadership skills necessary to convince an urban- and suburban-based Congress that the problems of farmers were worth solving.

From 1976 to 1985 the United States had returned to a system in which the government, not the marketplace, controlled food policy. Meanwhile the executive and legislative branches had lost leaders who simultaneously understood the farm sector and were capable leaders. By 1985 the governmental institutions responsible for making agricultural decisions were in disarray, and Washington experts had difficulty identifying the officials who really controlled America's food policy.

---

1. The restrictions were based on estimates. Later, when the estimates proved wrong and expenditures were much higher than anyone had believed possible, the restrictions of the 1981 budget process seemed academic. In 1981, however, the principal players behaved as if the restrictions were real.

Index